NGS

daism
tianity
nnings

Perelmuter

PAULIST PRESS
New York and Mahwah, N.J.

Paulist Press gratefully acknowledges the use of selections from the Soncino translation of the Talmud, reprinted by permission of The Soncino Press Limited, N.Y.

Library of Congress Cataloging-in-Publication Data

Perelmuter, Hayim Goren.
   Siblings : Rabbinic Judaism and early Christianity at their
beginnings / Hayim Goren Perelmuter.
     p.   cm.
   ISBN 0-8091-3104-8
   1. Judaism—History—Post-exilic period, 586 B.C.-210 A.D.
2. Tannaim.   3. Rabbinical literature—Translations into English.
I. Title.
BM176.P37   1989
296'.09'015—dc20   89-37643
                                                     CIP

Published by Paulist Press
997 Macarthur Boulevard
Mahwah, New Jersey 07430

Printed and bound in the
United States of America

Contents

For
Ben, Gabi and Jonathan

Acknowledgements

For the idea of this book and its completion I must acknowledge the gentle but persistent prodding of Lawrence Boadt, of the Paulist Press, who almost ten years ago first suggested that the course in Rabbinic Judaism I had been teaching at the Catholic Theological Union would be worth putting into a book.

His prodding was aided and abetted by the invitation of Clemens Thoma to give this course as a series of lectures in German at the Institut fuer juedisch-christliche Forschung in Luzern for the Fall-Winter semester of 1986. This invitation broke the camel's back of hesitation and I began to write down the lectures for translation, and thus came to see the possibilities for a book.

I am grateful also to Wilhelm Wuellner, at the Pacific School of Religion, who read the manuscripts in English and German, made useful suggestions, and urged me to go forward with the project; to the Soncino Press for permission to use extensive quotations; to Kenneth O'Malley, librarian of the Catholic Theological Union, for preparing the index; and to Ellis Rivkin for some valuable suggestions.

The Catholic Theological Union, where I have taught since 1968, has been a warm and creative environment to work over the years, as were the Pacific Lutheran Theological Seminary and the Graduate Theological Union, where I have taught spring semesters since 1980, and where a goodly portion of the writing was done.

Above all I am grateful to my wife Nancy, who particularly in Luzern proofread the work, for her many important suggestions for style and clarification, and for her general support, encouragement and love.

Introduction

This book is intended for those readers who are of the opinion that understanding the literature of Rabbinic Judaism is as difficult as finding a path through the mythical Cretan maze without Ariadne's thread.

Perhaps it will serve as a modest compass to guide the venturesome reader across the uncharted distances of what has been called the "Sea of the Talmud." The skilled navigator makes his or her way through calm or stormy weather with an aplomb that brings in its wake a safe harbor of understanding. The neophyte has a more difficult and perilous journey, but it can be undertaken.

This book is for the serious neophyte who has an intuition that Rabbinic Judaism which at once preceded and was contemporary with early Christianity needs to be understood both for itself and for a better understanding of the Christianity that evolved from it, parted from it, and in recent years has been animated by a deeply felt need to find its way back to its roots.

The genesis of this work is to be found in almost two decades of effort to teach an introductory course variously titled "Rabbinic Judaism and the Early Church," "A History of Rabbinic Exegesis and Preaching," and "The Texts and Textures of Jesus' Jewish Background" at the Catholic Theological Union at Chicago, the Graduate Theological Union and Pacific Lutheran Theological Seminary in Berkeley, the Institut fuer Juedisch-Christliche Forschung of Luzern, and the Evangelische Theologische Fakultaet of the University of Bern. Whatever the title, the goal was the same.

That goal was to provide an understanding of the development of Rabbinic Judaism through the medium of what I see to be eight central figures in its development using texts from the Talmud and the Midrash as the source material. Through this expedient the reader would follow the development and at the same time learn how to deal with Rabbinic texts through the medium of the existing translations.

The Soncino translations of the Talmud and the Midrash will be found to be especially useful because they both have excellent indexes which become an open sesame to the wide range of thematic material found all over its pages, and contain as well an index of scriptural quotations which can lead the reader to the talmudic and midrashic exegesis of almost any verse in the Jewish Scriptures.

Hopefully a second volume, tracing the history of Jewish preaching, will appear one day soon as a sequel to this volume.

From the very beginning, some twenty years ago, as I attempted to guide students into the world of Rabbinic Judaism, I rejected the view of conventional wisdom that Judaism was the parent faith and Christianity the child. The Rabbinic Judaism that shaped the journey into history after the destruction of the Jewish State was in a real sense a mutation designed for survival.

In its development from the fourth pre-Christian century until and beyond the year 70, when the Romans destroyed Jerusalem and sowed the seeds of the beginning of the end of the Second Jewish Commonwealth, this development of Rabbinic Judaism, with its emphasis on change linked to continuity, with its strong messianic sense and its deep belief in resurrection, was the common background of both normative Judaism and Christianity.

Both Rabbinic Judaism and early Christianity received their basic form at the same time, each placing a different reading of the messianic force at work within Judaism and the Jewish people. Thus they can be viewed as siblings, and it is this idea that suggested the title for this book.

I am fully aware of the fact that there are differences of opinion on this matter in the scholarly world. There are those who see the roots of Rabbinic Judaism and Pharisaism many centuries before the advent of Christianity. In fact I suggest the possibility of the time of Jeremiah with his letter to the Babylonian exiles, and the identification of Malachi with Ezra in a Targum commentary. And so it could be argued that this being the case, the Sibling argument falls of its own weight.

However, I find it persuasive to take the destruction of Jerusalem, and the reorganization around Yavneh on the one hand, and the appearance of the early gospels on the other, as two parallel responses to the destruction of Jerusalem and the State. It becomes for me a useful midrash against which the suggested sibling approach can be viewed.

The intention was to teach the process not through historical narrative or scholarly analysis of development, important though these may be, but rather through a direct confrontation with Rabbinic texts. In this way it became possible to derive both the process and the saga directly from them. Thus the connection with Rabbinic texts through Talmud and Midrash would be made easier and an entrance into the intellectual and spiritual world from which the siblings emerged made possible.

The first two chapters should be read to establish the parameters of the study. The process of *midrash,* and a swift recapitulation of Jewish history from its beginnings to the end of the Second Jewish Commonwealth will attempt to set the stage. Chapters Three through Eight will trace the development of Rabbinic Judaism through eight rabbinic figures from the first pre-Christian century to the end of the second century. These include Simeon ben Shetah, Hillel, Johanan ben Zakkai, Eliezer ben Hyrcanus, Joshua ben Hananiah, Akiba, Meir and Elisha ben Abuya. They are strange names as the reader begins the book. By the time the book is completed, they will be old and valued friends.

This study will conclude with an account of the development of the *derashah* or sermon as we find it in talmudic sources. It will show how the sermon can be viewed as a Jewish invention, growing out of the midrash form that was crafted by the development of rabbinic Judaism, and, in fact, became its technique for communicating the raison d'être to the people as a whole.

It will be helpful to read each chapter and then examine the rabbinic texts appended thereto. This will reinforce what has been read and at the same time quickly develop a feel for this genre of literature.

To mix mythological metaphors from one culture to another, which in a way is what this little book is about, this method may helpfully serve as a sort of "Ariadne's thread" to lead us out of the maze of confusion into a healthy awareness of how the siblings began.

Chapter One

Tale, Teller and Text

The story of Rabbinic Judaism, the history of Jewish preaching, and the relationship between Judaism and Christianity are, in a very profound sense, really one story. It is that one story that I propose to tell.

Rabbinic Judaism can be properly viewed as both a crucial mutation in the process we know as Jewish history, and as a crucial revolutionary technique that made possible the survival of the Judaism of the biblical period into that period of its history when there was no state, no land, no temple, no king, no priest, no prophet.

It was a way of transforming and transmuting all these, by the magic of *Midrash,* into a form of survival that made every single Jew a bearer of the whole process, and every little scattered community of as few as ten a symbol of the entire people, wherever they might be.

This study is an attempt to trace the development of Rabbinic/Pharisaic Judaism. It places its origins at the end of the First Jewish Commonwealth, its development during the Second Jewish Commonwealth, and its bifurcation thereafter into Long Range Messianic Judaism and Short Range Messianic Christianity. It will attempt to show Judaism and Christianity as siblings rather than in a parent-child relationship.

We shall take a close look at the development of this process through an examination, in the texts of Talmud and Midrash, of a group of rabbinic sages from the first pre-Christian century to the second post-Christian century. We shall examine at one and the same time the sibling relationship which they share in common, and the tension that separated them from each other. We shall also take a look at the rabbinic process we call *Midrash*, out of which emerged the hermeneutic that made the development of Judaism and Christianity possible.

First let us take a look at the word *Midrash* itself, for it is in this word and the process it represents that the central concept which explains Rabbinic Judaism is encapsulated. As we proceed we will discover in fuller detail how Rabbinic Judaism developed. For the present it is sufficient to understand that the crucial, revolutionary innovation of Rabbinic Judaism which made possible the survival of Judaism and the Jewish people out of the ashes of the destruction of Temple and State by the Romans into two thousand years of diaspora was this idea: that the central written teachings of Judaism encompassed in the Torah needed at once to be preserved and changed.

How could this possibly be done, given the central role of the Sinaitic revelation to the whole purpose of Jewish existence? The answer was to be found in the revolutionary concept that at Mount Sinai there were two simultaneous revelations and not one. There was the Written Torah and the Oral Torah. Both were simultaneously revealed and both had equal status. The Oral Torah interpreted the Written Torah. And the process of interpretation was known as *Midrash*.

The word *Midrash* means "interpretation" or "hermeneutic process." It is the central process of Rabbinic Judaism. It is the one process more than any other that is the key to the understanding of Judaism. It comes from the Hebrew root *darash* which means to "seek," "search," "exegete." From it we derive the name of the person who does the exegeting or interpreting—the term *darshan*. This has come to be the Hebrew word for "preacher" or "homilist." But it is the process of *Midrash* which concerns us at this time.

Let us take several fundamental principles and conceptions in Judaism to see how the process works. There is, for example, the principle that change within continuity is a fundamental process within Judaism. There is the principle that majority rule must prevail in the decision making process in the Sanhedrin, the Supreme Court of Jewish Law. There is the theological premise that Torah is at the very basis of everything that exists. And, finally, how principles like freedom and the role of the individual as God's witness in the human enterprise become both implicit and exegeted theological principles of Judaism.

For example, it has already been suggested that a central thesis of Rabbinic Judaism would have it that change in the development of Judaism, change linked to continuity, was crucial. Nowhere do we find this stated as an operative principle. It is stated by what is done, and the principle is affirmed—where else?—in a *Midrash*.

The Jew came to read the Bible through the lens of Rabbinic interpretation. Rabbinic imagination and insight constantly deepened the understanding of the text and provided new insights through flights of imagination.

Without any further ado, let us leap boldly into several *Midrashim* so that we can get a feel for this Rabbinic process that will be at the center of our concern. It is necessary to do this, for unlike the Greek intellectual system, and the system of medieval Christianity, both of which set forth their positions in structured statements of philosophy or theology, the Rabbinic method was neither structured nor linear. Theology in Judaism was implicit in *Midrash*, and through it was always stated by indirection.

In the book of Deuteronomy the death of Moses is very briefly and very succinctly described. God tells him that his time has come to die, and he in fact goes up to the mountain and does die. In the biblical narrative there is not the least hint of a struggle. And the tale ends with the statement that Moses died in the fullness of his powers, and that no prophet like him has arisen since.

But this is not sufficient for the Rabbinic sages. They developed a vast range of speculation of what went on at the time that death was about to come to this greatest of humans, according to Scripture, who had ever lived. Moses resists death, and demands, because of what he had been through with the people, the right to enter the Promised Land. He defies the Angel of Death sent to carry out the orders. God finally finds it necessary to intervene, and after persuading Moses to submit, takes his life with a kiss!

God achieves this goal by reasoning with Moses. The account of this struggle as we find it in the *Midrash* is resolved by Moses' acquiescence, according to the sages, when God in effect says to Moses: "Look, Moses, I know that the real reason you are reluctant to die is that you are uncertain what will happen to this people you led out of Egypt at My direction. If I can assure you that everything will turn out well in the end, that there will be a succession of competent leaders, will that satisfy you?" Moses nods in assent. [cf. Supplement: Akiba #1]

To achieve this, the *Midrash* tells us, God projects Moses forward in time a thousand years and shows him Akiba, the greatest teacher of his age, teaching the essence of Judaism to thousands of his disciples. Moses sits in this huge class listening. To his great dismay and horror he does not understand a word that is being taught! He is totally at a loss, totally confused. Was this the Torah he had brought down from Sinai? Was this what he had taught the people? The *Midrash* tells us that his face grew dark with dismay and anger until the following event occurs:

One student gets up and puts a question to the Master. "Master," he says, "from whence do you deduce this teaching?" To which Akiba, the Akiba who takes the first crucial steps in the organization of the Oral Laws so that they ultimately emerged as Mishnah, replies: "*Halakhah l'Moshe miSinai*—It is according to the teachings of Moses at Sinai!"

Hearing this, Moses' face lit up and he heaved a sigh of relief. He had not understood a word that was being taught, but it was being taught in his name! He could then say to God: "Now I am ready to die."

The Sages were not interested just in telling an amusing tale in connection with this *Midrash*. They were making a point, a serious theological point. They were showing that change and continuity were linked together closely, that change indeed was the guarantee of continuity, that change did not alter the essence, but without it life could not go on.

What about the struggle for democracy?

For this we go to the year 90. The Romans have destroyed Jerusalem. Rabbinic Judaism is already taking form. Christianity is also developing. The first Gospels are already circulating. The center of Jewish authority, the Sanhedrin, is now in the hands of the Rabbi/Sages. Eliezer ben Hyrcanus, a land-owning patrician and the greatest authority of his time in the unwritten traditions, heads the Sanhedrin. He is convinced that since he knows more than anyone else, he should be the supreme authority to decide ultimate issues.

His antagonist is Joshua ben Hananiah. Joshua is a man of the people. He believes in collegiality, that is to say, that a majority consensus should have the final say. He leads the opposition with persistence and intelligence and finally wins the day. There is a coup, and Eliezer is unseated and excommunicated because of his intransigence. In consequence of this, the democratic principle is established in the Sanhedrin. [cf. Supplement: Eliezer ben Hyrcanus #5]

But that is not the way it is recorded. We get this development through a story/*Midrash*. In the Babylonian Talmud, in the Tractate *Baba Mezia*, which deals principally with matters of civil law, there is a discussion about authority in declaring an object ritually clean or unclean. The issue at hand happened to be whether a certain oven was ritually unclean or not. Eliezer, we are told, ruled it ritually clean, but his colleagues would not accept his opinion.

Becoming irritated, he thought he would really show the dissenters that he was right by invoking a miracle. Surely that would persuade them. So he said: "Let this carob tree jump ten feet to prove me right." And would you believe it, it did just that! But they would not accept this evidence. His irritation grew. "To prove that I am right," he continued, "let this stream of water flow uphill." And it did just that! But the colleagues remained unconvinced. His irritation grew. "The walls of this hall of study will prove me right," he cried, and the walls began to totter. At this point Joshua intervened, crying out: "O walls, what business is it of yours when scholars argue?" So the walls did not collapse, the narrative continues, out of respect for Rabbi Joshua, nor did they straighten up because of Eliezer, and to this day, the story continues with a straight face, the walls are slanted.

Eliezer had had enough. He would play his biggest card. Turning to his colleagues, he cried out: "I call upon a *Bath Kol* [i.e. a voice from heaven] to prove me right." And a voice from heaven indeed spoke up and said: "My children, everything that Rabbi Eliezer has said is correct. The *halakhah* is as he says."

Thereupon Joshua leaped to his feet and cried out: "The decision is not in heaven! For since the Torah was given to Moses it contains the principle 'after the majority one must incline' " [Exodus 23:2]. What a startling way to assert the democratic principle! What an extraordinary way to report a crucial turning, the development of authority in Judaism. And it is done with a tale that is a midrash, a midrash based on a phrase in Moses' farewell address, and a phrase from the legal code in Exodus.

The teller of the tale here realizes that something extraordinary has happened. God, it would appear, has been defied. Is this not a heresy of heresies?

The story goes on. After this unusual event, Rabbi Nathan who had been present at the episode encounters the prophet Elijah. Elijah has been dead some eight hundred years, so what is he doing in a Talmudic story? It needs to be understood that by this time Elijah the Prophet, long dead, had become a mythical figure in Jewish tradition. He had come to be seen as the prophet who would return on the eve of the eschaton and the advent of the Messiah, to announce the impending event. That is how Malachi, the last of the prophets, ends his message. That is why this Christian version of Hebrew Scripture ends with Malachi. In the Talmud Elijah is the one who, in the end of time, will solve all dialectical problems raised by the Sages.

When a problem would seem to be insoluble, the Talmud was wont to say *teku*, a Hebrew acronym for *Tishbi yitaretz kushiyot v'abayot* [Elijah will solve all unsolved problems]. At the Seder table on Passover, a fifth cup was placed for Elijah, the harbinger of redemption. The chair upon which the Jewish male child was held by a sponsor when he was circumcised was known as Elijah's Chair, because of the hope that this child might turn out to be the Messiah. At the end of the Sabbath at *havdalah*, the ceremony of separation of the Holy from the Weekday, the presence of Elijah was always invoked.

Moreover, everywhere in the Talmud and post-talmudic

tales, Elijah appears out of nowhere, to let us know what went on in the heavenly spheres, or what some occult event means.

Thus telling the tale of Eliezer's defeat, and Joshua's defiance of God in the spirit of Abraham on the question of Sodom and Gomorrah, and Jeremiah's challenge to God on the suffering of the righteous, and the apparent rewards of the wicked, a shocking episode on the face of it, the story continues:

> Rabbi Nathan met Elijah [after this event] and asked him: What did the Holy One Blessed Be He do at that moment? He laughed with joy [came Elijah's answer] and replied: My sons have defeated me, my sons have defeated me.

Thus a momentous milestone in the development of Rabbinic Judaism is recorded as a landmark event—not soberly and somberly but with a Midrash, related tongue in cheek, and no less aware despite the humor that an enormous step forward had been taken. The cause of democracy and collegiality had won the day.

Thus far we have looked at Midrash as it expresses the Rabbinic attitude to change qua change, and to the democratic principle in arriving at conclusions. Let us take a look at a third category to see the traces of theological development.

For Rabbinic Judaism written and oral Torah alike have the Sinaitic stamp of authenticity. Torah as revealed to Moses in all its implications and as exegeted by the sages is central—so central, in fact, that it pre-existed in the scheme of divine creation. And to speak of anything pre-existing, when Judaism is founded on the rock of *creatio ex nihilo,* would seem to border on the heretical. Yet Rabbinic Judaism makes this statement to underscore the absolute centrality of Torah in the scheme of things.

The sages have no time for nonsense. They begin at the beginning. They look at the very first words of the Torah: *Bereshit bara Elohim et hashmayimv'et ha'aretz* [In the beginning God created the heaven and the earth]. Does *bereshit* really mean *in the beginning*? Nonsense, was their reply. It should rather be rendered as "God created heaven and earth with *Reshit*]. And to your question, "What is *reshit*?" they reply, "To understand what *Reshit* really means you must look at Proverbs 8:22 where the text reads: *Adonay kanani reshit darko* [God acquired me the first of His way]. Wisdom is speaking here, and Wisdom is obviously Torah, and it is described as the "first" of God's way. Obviously it existed before anything else was created!

Hence we are to understand the opening sentence of the Torah as saying: "With *reshit* [i.e. Torah] God created the heaven and the earth." Thus through this skillful *midrash,* the sages affirm the idea that the Torah was so central that it was created before the world was created, that it was, in fact, an underlying force of the creative process [Midrash, Genesis Rabbah 1:1].

An exegetical act of legerdemain that transforms the meaning of a word becomes the foundation stone of the theological structure that emerges. Let us take a quick look at two others.

Everybody would say that the Hebrew word *berakhah* means blessing. For example, when Abraham makes his appearance on the stage of history as the first spokesperson for the One, Universal God, this God says to him, at the very beginning: *heyay berakhah* [be thou a blessing]. Is that what it means? Blessing? If not "blessing" then what is God telling Abraham to be?

Very simple, say the Sages. The secret is in the four Hebrew consonants: *bet, resh, kaph, he.* Since the Torah is written without vowels, we need not accept the massoretic vowels. If a vowel changes it provides not only better meaning, but clearer understanding. "Do not read the word *berakhah*" [blessing], they advise us, "rather read it *berekhah* [well of water]" [Midrash, Genesis Rabbah, 39:11].

Here then is what God is saying to Abraham: "Be like a well of water." This desert-schooled Abraham, as did his desert-schooled descendants, knew full well that a well of water in the desert, an oasis, is the greatest possible blessing we can have. How then can Abraham "be a blessing"? By being spiritually life-giving to humanity around him as is an oasis in the desert, which is a source of life in the midst of death.

Thus, suggest the Sages, when we say "baruch atta Adonay" we are saying not, "blessed are You, Adonay", but rather,

"Adonay, you are to us like an oasis in the desert!" Here indeed is an insight into the theology of blessing.

One final *midrash* in this last group of theological insights: After the episode of the Golden Calf, and the shattering of the Tablets, there is a new revelation to Moses. Here the text in Exodus speaks of the commandments with these words: *harut b'etzba Elohim* [graven with the finger of God]—a noble image indeed not only of divine inspiration, but of divine execution, as well. But the Sages are not satisfied with this. "Do not read the word *harut* [engraved]; rather read it *herut* [freedom]." They wanted to say that true freedom lay in giving oneself to Torah, that study of Torah was indeed a liberating force [Babylonian Talmud, Erubin 54a].

Midrash, you see, is deemed central. A fourteenth century popular preacher builds on an interpretation of a fourth century Sage. This Sage in turn comments on a prophet who lived a full seven hundred years before the Christian era, in order to make the point crisply, clearly and unequivocally [cf. Babylonian Talmud, Hagigah 14a].

Rav Dimi, a fourth century *amora,* of whom it was said that he was not endowed with worldly goods but was blessed with a good conscience, took his text from Isaiah 3:1–4:

> For behold the Lord, the Lord of hosts, doth take away
> from Jerusalem and from Judah stay and staff, every
> stay of bread and every stay of water.

From this text he deduced the whole range of Jewish learning. This verse, he suggested, means that God will punish the people in the most severe way, by depriving them of their teachers. "Stay," he suggested, refers to masters of the Bible, "staff" to masters of the Mishnah, "bread" to masters of the Talmud and "water" [remember *berakhah?*], masters of *agadah.* The fourteenth century preacher from Spain, Isaac Aboab, expands on this interpretation with the words:

> Just as man in his diet requires bread some of the time
> and water all of the time to keep the body alive, to keep

the soul alive you require the *mitzvot* [commandments] at fixed times and *agadot* [homilies] at all times [cf. Isaac Aboab, *Menorat haMaor* folio 3b, Vilna 1851].

So we see how central the *midrash* process is seen to be. And *agadah*, the telling of the tale that is exegeted, is given a paramount role. Tale, text and teller are inextricably linked in the development of Rabbinic Judaism, and it is our purpose to explore the process through a group of central figures, from the third pre-Christian century to the third post-Christian century, who develop and communicate that process.

Early Christianity can best be understood against this background. Here too *midrash* can be seen to play a significant role.

In reading *midrash*, and the preachers who have used it, we come across a fairly frequent phenomenon. Very often the *midrash* will quote the first half of the verse but base its interpretation on the second half. It was assumed that the listener knew it. If this were not the case, it would be very hard to understand what the speaker was talking about. But the preacher assumed, and in most instances quite correctly, that he was speaking to an audience steeped in scripture. They could complete the sentence very much like an audience responding to a charismatic speaker.

Applying this method to the New Testament account of the last words of Jesus on the cross, the unforgettable words *"Eloi, Eloi, lama zabachtani"* ["My God, my God, why have you forsaken me?"] we can come to a startling conclusion. We can suggest that this is not a cry of despair, but rather a clarion call of hope. With these three words, Jesus was really saying to the people: "Psalm 22!" He was sure they would know it. They would know that it began with a cry of despair, and ended on a note of exultant hope and confidence in God:

Then the meek shall eat and be satisfied; those who seek Him shall praise the Lord! May your hearts be revived forever! All the ends of the earth shall remember and turn to the Lord.

Jesus, after all, was a *darshan* par excellence, and *midrash*, in which he had been raised and nurtured was here speaking through him out of his deep Jewish roots. The process of *midrash*, this development, will be our quest.

Chapter Two

Christianity and Judaism as Siblings

Conventional wisdom would have it that Judaism is the parent and that Christianity is the child. In considering the great religions of the western world, we often hear both Christianity and Islam described as "daughter faiths" of Judaism. This is certainly correct on the assumption that both faiths derive from the Bible. Both Christian and Moslem vie with the Jew in claiming authentic patrimony from Abraham.

We have already seen, however, how Rabbinic or Pharisaic Judaism represented a significant mutation in the development of the Jewish experience. We have viewed Rabbinic/Pharisaic Judaism as a revolution, introducing the conception of change for the sake of continuity.

Rabbinic/Pharisaic Judaism represented a radical departure. New patterns for the organization of the Jewish people and Judaism came into being. In one way, the new was radically different from the old. And yet in another sense, it was a continuation of the old. Without the new the old would have died. In fact, in a sense, the old did die.

Both Rabbinic Judaism, the form in which Judaism survived the destruction of State and Temple by the Romans, and Christianity were shaped at approximately the same time. The shaping of the emerging pattern for the survival of Judaism came out of Yavneh, at just about the same time the first gospels were written to crystallize the new Christianity.

Indeed we can look at it this way: The conflict between Rome and Judea was a struggle that lasted almost two hundred years. A friendly Rome, following its principle of *divide et impera* [divide and rule] had befriended the Maccabean guerrillas to weaken the Seleucids and the Egyptians. That made possible the emergence of the Second Jewish Commonwealth as an independent state.

However, by 42 B.C.E., the silk gloves came off, the iron fist showed, and Pompey's troops occupied Judea. The resistance developed into a series of brutal wars, out of which Rome emerged victorious, but bloodied. Nowhere else in her military experience had she encountered such resistance.

In their confrontation with Rome the Jewish people had five options:

They could assimilate, and become Roman. Many of their predecessors had done just that during the Hellenistic period. Many did so again. In fact, the nephew of Philo, Tiberias Alexander, became thoroughly Romanized, joined the army, rose in the ranks, and was second-in-command to Titus when Jerusalem was destroyed in the year 70.

They could decide to fight to the death. The slogan might have been: "Better dead than Roman!" This was the path chosen by the Zealots. Betar was its grisly consequence of mass death and destruction, and Masada its somber memorial.

They could decide to withdraw from the world and resign from the struggle. They could retire to desert fastnesses there to wait for a better and redemptive day. This was the way of Qumran.

There were two other alternatives. These were implicit in the approach of Rabbinic/Pharisaic Judaism, which had already taken shape, and which thought in terms of survival through the messianic impulse that had developed within Judaism. Both alternatives came out of Rabbinic Judaism. Both were animated by a messianic thrust, but both thought in terms of survival and not of suicide. The one believed the messianic time was at hand and should be grasped boldly. The other, having seen the messianic impulse take the form of military resistance that failed disastrously, took a long range view.

The short range messianic movement out of Judaism became Christianity. The long range messianic movement became Rabbinic Judaism. The former plunged headlong into the world of the Roman Empire, and "conquered" it in less than two centuries. The latter signed a temporary "cease fire" with Rome, and within those same two centuries moved out of the sphere of the Roman Empire, into the Parthian Empire. There perhaps a million Jews lived, where they developed Rabbinic Judaism by expanding Mishnah into Talmud, and returning into Europe as fully developed Judaism by the eighth century. It was, to quote the French, *reculer pour mieux sauter* [taking one step back the better to leap forward].

It is in this sense that Judaism and Christianity are clearly siblings, both responding to the same cataclysmic event, as Jews, but each taking a different approach to the messianic destiny.

A word here is in place to explain the rapid growth of Christianity within the Roman Empire. For one thing, there was a spiritual crisis in all of the Empire. The old ways were failing. For another, there were many Jews all over the Empire.

It has been estimated by historical demographers that the total population of the Roman Empire was sixty million. Of these, six million were Jews, about half in Judea and the other half in the rest of the Empire. One in ten were Jews. We have evidence from Roman sources that Judaism was beginning to make inroads among the Romans. The references to the *yir'ei Adonay* [those who fear God], known among the Romans as *metuentes*, are an indication of this. It is estimated that the growth of the Jewish population received an impulse from the Phoenecians in North Africa and Spain after the defeat by the Romans in the Punic Wars in the second pre-Christian century. The Phoenecians were Hebrew speaking—or, you might prefer to say, the Jews spoke Phoenecian. It is surmised that after defeat and being cut off from their homeland, they merged with the Jewish communities around the Empire.

In any event there were great centers of Jewish population all over the Roman Empire. The explosion of revolts all over at the time of the Bar Cochba revolt in 135 bears witness to this. By way of example, Alexandria was the first ancient city to attain a population of a million. It is estimated that that million was made up of three hundred thousand Egyptians, three hundred thousand Greeks, and three hundred thousand Jews. Evidence of Jewish influence was widespread. Juvenal, in showing how par-

ents corrupted their children, could speak of one such who had a
father who observed the Sabbath. Christian instant messianic
missionaries indeed had fertile soil to cultivate. It is no wonder
that the movement spread with lightning speed. After all, this
significant presence of Jews scattered through the Roman Empire constituted the primary soil from which the new seed
sprouted.

We have already spoken of the tension between instant messianism and long range messianism in the Introduction. For the
present it will suffice to look at one piece of evidence—the arrangement of the Hebrew Scriptures by the early Synagogue
and the early Church.

Both groups, from the matrix of Rabbinic/Pharisaic Judaism,
looked on the Bible as their sacred primary resource. In the Jewish arrangement, Pentateuch was followed by Prophetic Books
which were followed by the *Ketubim* [Writings]. The Jewish arrangement ends with the Book of Chronicles. The Christian arrangement placed the Prophetic Books at the end, because these
ended with Malachi, and Malachi ended with the words:

> Lo, I will send the prophet Elijah to you before the
> coming of the awesome, fearful day of the Lord. [Mala-
> chi 3:23]

This surely was an appropriate link between Old Testament and
New, and it was an eloquent testimony of the conviction that the
Messiah had come. It was an affirmation of the instant messianic
thesis within Rabbinic Judaism.

The arrangement as canonized at Yavneh by Rabbinic Judaism, the arrangement of the sacred scriptures for Jews, ends with
the Second Book of Chronicles. Here are the concluding words:

> And in the first year of King Cyrus of Persia, when the
> word of the Lord spoken by Jeremiah was fulfilled, the
> Lord roused the spirit of King Cyrus of Persia to issue a
> proclamation throughout his realm by word of mouth
> and in writing, as follows: "Thus said King Cyrus of
> Persia: The Lord God of Heaven has given me all the

kingdoms of the earth, and has charged me with building Him a House in Jerusalem, which is in Judah. Any
one of you of all His people, the Lord God be with him
and let him go up. [2 Chronicles 36:22ff]

So here we have it. The siblings equally impelled by their
scriptural and messianic roots blaze new trails in the highways of
history, starting from a common origin and moving forward in
diverse routes. We must remember the Jeremiah mentioned in
Chronicles, for he is, in my view, central to the development of
Rabbinic Judaism whence both siblings emerge. But first let us
sketch, with swift and rapid strokes, the common history of the
siblings that represented their common background.

It will be helpful if we view the history preceding the parting
of the ways between Church and Synagogue in the second century as three six hundred year segments. If we date Abraham at
approximately 1800 BCE and the Exodus from Egypt at about
1200 BCE, we have our first segment. This marks the beginning,
as our common ancestor sets out to witness to the One God of
Humanity, assured of God's Promise and a Promised Land.

We have here the beginnings of nation and covenant, the
period of the patriarchs, the development of the clan, and, at the
very beginnings, the combination of experiences that become a
paradigm for Jewish historical experience—arrival at a homeland, diaspora, success, then failure, then return home.

When you stop to think of it, this period includes a first
encounter with God, beginnings, nationhood fashioned in exile,
and then return. What begins with commitment to God and
God's promise ends with God's fulfillment of that promise and
the return of the people to the Promised Land. The result provides material for memories of that encounter, for memories of
the beginnings, and for memories of the pause on the way home
at Sinai to renew the Covenant that was the outcome of that first
encounter. And this time it is not the experience of one patriarch
alone, but rather of the entire people.

What we have here, if you will, is the first struggle for freedom, the first national liberation movement in all historic experience, and the first messianic experience, a fulfilled messianic ex-

perience for the Jewish people. These then are the beginnings, and here the basic themes of Jewish history are established.

Now for the second six hundred years from 1200 BCE [approximately] to 600 BCE [approximately]. This period takes us from the settlement of the land, the development of the first Jewish Commonwealth, to the destruction of Jerusalem by the Babylonians [586 BCE], and the exile to Babylonia. Here Jewish covenant nationhood comes to its completest fulfillment and fruition. Here the patriarchal period of Beduin-type wandering, tribal organization, oscillation between promised land and diaspora, individual covenant, group covenant, exile and messianic return become embodied in the physical trappings of state, of Temple, of national religious institutions.

The state grows and develops, and the covenant memories as well. This is the period that produces Temple and priesthood, sanctioned by God, monarchy and kingship, sanctioned by God. It produces as well something else, and something unique: the embodiment of that special kind of communication between the newly discovered one, universal God and the special vessels of the communication of His message through an Abraham, a Moses and finally an entire consecrated God-dedicated people. This embodiment we call prophet, and that which the prophets were about we call prophecy.

Prophets are the embodied conscience of the people, the crucial means of communication between God and His covenant people. There is ample need for this communication, for the people and its leaders, despite the best of intentions, are always forgetting and always tending to go astray. It is the prophets who are the visible, ever present, and ever uncomfortable prod. It is the prophets whose hand guides the editing of scripture. The historical and prophetic books are clear evidence of this. All of Jewish history up to that point is to be remembered from their point of view. The greatest events not relevant to their point of view were simply omitted. Witness the great achievements of Jeroboam II and the remarkably little space he gets in the Book of Kings, despite them!

Temple and cult attain the high and magnificent and impressive solemnity of the Sanctuary in Jerusalem; monarchy culminates in the glories of the Davidic dynasty; but after all is said and done, the legacy of the First Jewish Commonwealth is neither a Jewish-type acropolis nor a Jewish type complex of palaces, pyramids, or soaring obelisks. It is rather the prophetic heritage that becomes the Bible for us. Pentateuch, prophets, some psalms and some of the other books are products of this period. The prophets place their stamp on the spirit of these books, and on the heritage they design for the people to preserve. Simply put, if you were to add the century or so that followed the destruction of the first Temple, this is the period that provides us with the Tanakh [Old Testament as it is named in the Christian world], the first great literary creation of this period.

When this period comes to an end, and it comes to an end with a catastrophic upheaval, it leaves the national hopes in ashes, leaves the survivors to pick up the pieces: putting together their literary heritage—the Bible; organizing their memories—Davidic dynasty and its glories; remembering the Temple and its magnificence.

This catastrophe has a numbing but not a paralyzing effect. "How can we sing a song of the Lord on alien soil?" [Psalms 137:4] the exiles asked, and yet they did. The Book of Lamentations describes the numbing trauma: "Bitterly she weeps in the night . . . there is none to comfort her." [Lam. 1:2] The people recall: "All the precious things she had in the days of old, Jerusalem recalled in her days of woe and sorrow." [Lam. 1:7]; they remember and they do something about preserving the memories. In the aftermath of catastrophe a superhuman effort to collect and preserve the written memories of the days of glory goes forward, probably most especially in Babylonia. Out of this we get the edited Pentateuch, the histories and most of the prophetic books. And we get Jeremiah, the Jeremiah I have already mentioned.

I focus on Jeremiah because, in my view, it is in Jeremiah and what he does that we see the first seeds of what becomes the flower of Rabbinic Judaism.

Jeremiah is the prophet who witnesses the destruction. He has desperately tried to prevent it. As God's reluctant spokesman he was constant—and how he suffered for it—in his message that in obedience to God and His ways, and not in pragmatic political alliances, lay the path to survival and the avoidance of destruction. But no one listens to him. Those who support regional military alliances against Babylonia, especially with Egypt, carry the day. Their failures result in the siege of Jerusalem and its ultimate destruction.

While Jerusalem is already in flames, and the end in sight, Jeremiah does two things. He buys a plot of land in Jerusalem to express the faith that there will be a future, that "houses and fields and vineyards shall yet again be bought in this land." [Jer. 32:15] And he writes a letter to the exiles in Babylonia who are being assured by the people whom Jeremiah opposes that the exile will be of short duration, and he tells them:

> Build houses and live in them, plant gardens and eat
> their fruit. Take wives and beget sons and daughters;
> and take wives for your sons, and give your daughters
> to husbands, that they may bear sons and daughters.
> Multiply there, do not decrease. And seek the welfare
> of the city to which I have exiled you, and pray to the
> Lord in its behalf; for in its prosperity you shall pros-
> per. [Jer. 29:5ff]

Here, for the first time, we have the expression of the long range messianic outlook as contrasted with the impatience of its short range exponents, who were proclaiming a swift and early redemption.

As it turned out, the restoration came neither as quickly as the prophets opposing Jeremiah would have it, nor as slowly as Jeremiah himself predicted. But he was already projecting a strategy for Jewish survival that took account of the real possibility of destruction. In a sense, with respect to the Second Commonwealth that was to follow, he was giving the cure in advance of the disease!

For in setting a permanent community in Babylonia, he set up an area for developments in Judaism that looked to new possibilities for survival. And there was coming into being a great center of Jewish life, where the long range messianists, after the destruction of the Second Commonwealth could retreat, as I have already said, and where Rabbinic Judaism could go forward and develop.

For in the period between the destruction by Babylonia, and the beginnings of restoration under Ezra, a period of a scant century or so, we have the end of the prophetic period and the beginning of the transition of Rabbinic Judaism.

With Ezra we get the Men of the Great Synagogue. The reading of the Torah was introduced into the prayer life of the Jewish people, even though the Temple was being rebuilt. The process of *midrash* was introduced and that has already been touched upon. There evolved generations of sages who developed the Oral Law, and transformed the teachings of the prophets and the ways of the Temple cult into new ways that could survive destruction. It was not without significance that an early Aramaic translator of the Prophets could comment: "Malachi and Ezra are one person." [Targum Jonathan to Malachi 1:1] That is to say, the last prophet and the first of the Scribes/Sages/Pharisees were one!

Now the third six hundred years: This is the period of the Second Jewish Commonwealth. This is a period of rich and seminal creativity. It is a period of extraordinary pluralism and variety. Different sects surface in Judaism—Pharisee, Sadducee and Essene. We have gnostics and mystics, Hellenists and secularists. This is the time that the Middle East and the Greek world of Europe meet in an explosion of creativity, occasioned by their encounter.

Alexander the Great's sweep to the shores of India created an encounter between two ancient worlds. The challenge of Greek thought and Greek ways forced all the ancient cultures to reexamine and reevaluate themselves, and the development of Judaism was no exception. There are many who see the rapid development of Rabbinic Judaism in this period as a response to that challenge.

Suffice to say, this period of restoration is characterized by the Jewish people's confrontation not with Egypt, Babylonia, Assyria and Persia as in the past, but with Greece and Rome. Out of this came the final restoration of Jewish independence with the Maccabean revolt in 163 BCE. But underpinning it was an immense range of cultural and spiritual development as I have already indicated.

The transition from Biblical to Rabbinic mold of Judaism is quiet and imperceptible, but inexorable. You hardly see it develop. Yet when the Maccabean Revolt explodes, there is a people responding to a direction of leadership that is clearly a transition from the previous era of glory. The state is there again, but no Davidic dynasty. The Temple is there again but not in its former glory. There are prophets no longer. Now there are Rabbinic sages who are their heirs, and who give leadership and direction.

This is the period in which the Bible is completed, the period in which it is translated into Greek and carried to the Greek world. This is the period, as the Roman threat to independence sets in, that sees an explosion in messianic and eschatological thinking and writing. This is the period when an Aristotle can look upon Jews as a nation of philosophers, and Philo interprets Judaism to a Greek world steeped in Homer, Plato and Aristotle. This is the period when mystical groups explore the gnostic secrets, when Rabbinic interpretation expands the parameters of Torah.

Above all, these six hundred years saw the kinds of development in Judaism, with its messianic thrust and its capacity for survival, that created the subsoil out of which Rabbinic Judaism and Christianity grew. These six hundred years see the completion of the Bible, the Apocrypha, and end with the writing down of the Mishnah, the code of Oral laws, and the beginnings of the Siddur, the Prayer Book. The tools for survival and the crucial infrastructure were in place.

You may have noted how frequently the term Scribe/Sage/Pharisee has been used. This is to underscore the idea that they are interchangeable and represent the same thing. For it was out of the combination of scribe/sage/exegete that the type known as Rabbi, and called by their enemies Pharisee, emerges as the decisive developing type who shaped Judaism and the beginnings of Christianity. Already in Jeremiah's time we have the scribe Baruch. We have the scribe Ezra. Their role is to record and to teach. For Judaism is a text-bound destiny, bound to the Torah, its interpretation and expansion.

The characteristic of this Scribe/Sage/Rabbi/Pharisee model is that of teacher-exegete. The relationship and communication mode is teacher-disciple. The central principle is that the power over the text is not in an elite priesthood, but potentially available to every single Jew no matter what his status. The principle enunciated by the Rabbis that "a bastard who is a scholar outranks a High Priest who is an ignoramus" is clearly indicative of the direction. [Babylonian Talmud, Horayot 13a]

Before the time of Ezra, the Torah was the exclusive possession of the priests, and was read to the people once every seven years. With Ezra, the Torah is taken out of that exclusive domain, and read every week, so that by the end of the year it would all have been read. And not just read. It was read *m'forash*, interpreted, explained. The book of Nehemiah tells us how this happened the first time: "They read from the scroll of the Teaching of God, translating it and giving it sense, so they understood the reading." [Neh. 8:8]

"Translating and giving the sense so they understood. . . ." Here in a nutshell is the crux of Rabbinic Judaism. Here was seen how midrash is at the core, the process of explanation and of exegesis which was the theme of our first lecture. The Rabbinic Sage was truly a "novum," a mutation in history that seized a past, made it its own and handed it on to future generations.

Thus we see how in the turmoil surrounding the First Jewish Commonwealth this new phenomenon comes into being. We see how in the early days of the Second Commonwealth it begins to develop. We see how during the period of the Second Commonwealth it emerges full blown, fully prepared to step into the breach when this Commonwealth falls and the Jewish people enters its two thousand year diaspora period.

The *Pirkei Avot*, [the Ethics of the Fathers in the Mishnah] captures this development, and that is why it was placed at the beginning of the handbook that presented the generations of the Rabbinic Leaders who were the bridge of one period into the other. Here is what it tells us:

Moses received the Torah on Sinai and handed it down
to Joshua; Joshua to the elders; the elders to the prophets; and the prophets handed it down to the Men of the
Great Assembly. . . . Simon the Just was one of the last
survivors of the Men of the Great Assembly. . . . Antigonos of Socho received the tradition from Simon the
Just. . . . Jose the son of Yoezer of Zereda and Jose the
son of Yochanan received the tradition from the preceding. . . . Joshua the son of Perachya and Nittai the
Arbelite received the tradition from them. . . . Judah
ben Tabbai and Simeon the son of Shatach received the
tradition from them. . . . [Pirkei Avot 1:1]

And so it goes, down the generations. This list takes us from
the time of Ezra about 400 BCE to Simeon the son of Shetach
who lived approximately 100 BCE. And it is with this Simeon
that we shall begin to examine the crucial figures who shaped
Rabbinic Judaism, by developing its system and its means of
communication.

Chapter Three

Simeon ben Shetah

We shall be examining the development of Rabbinic Judaism through its hermeneutic, midrashic and exegetical process. This process involves a close scrutiny of some key personalities, and an examination of messianism, instant and long range, as twin forces. There is good reason for this because Rabbinic Judaism and the messianic thrust within it was the soil out of which diaspora Judaism and early Christianity were nurtured and grew.

Simeon ben Shetah is the first to be examined. He flourished in the first pre-Christian century. He was an interesting man. Stubborn and persistent for one thing. Resourceful for another. He was innovative to a high degree, and close to power, a power which he resisted, at the risk of his life. And in resisting it, he made possible the survival of Rabbinic Judaism. Close to power? It was not possible to get much closer. His sister was the wife of the King, Alexander Jannai.

It is no exaggeration to compare Simeon ben Shetah with Elijah who flourished eight centuries earlier. We remember Elijah's role, when the prophets of Baal assumed dominance, and when Jezebel, wife of Ahab, was Queen of Israel. She caused the destruction of all the prophets, and Elijah alone survived to resist their efforts to impose Baal worship upon all of Israel. But for him, the end would have come to the journey which began with Abraham and climaxed at Mount Sinai with the revelation of the Torah.

Who can forget Elijah's contest with the five hundred priests of Baal, and how he triumphed. It was one of those watershed moments in the human experience. Elijah emerged victorious, and the light of prophetic inspiration, bearing within it the survival of Judaism was not extinguished. But for Elijah, there might have been no Judaism.

In Judaism we have some very important "but for whoms." Abraham was one; Moses another. Simeon ben Shetah very much belongs in this category. Let us see why.

It has already been asserted that the mutation of Rabbinic Judaism was the crucial factor in making possible the survival of Judaism after the trauma of the destruction of the First Jewish State. Jeremiah and Ezra have been perceived as crucial elements in the transition. The pharisaic/rabbinic leaders who emerged from what they began did their work, quietly and imperceptibly, through the technique of their oral and written Torah systems and the process of *Midrash*.

What was going on in effect was a struggle for power between the pharisaic/rabbinic group on the one hand, and the priesthood and secular rulers on the other. The former won the hearts of the masses of the people, and in this reality we can understand where the power came for the victory of the Maccabean revolt and the ultimate establishment of the Second Commonwealth.

Like Elijah, Simeon ben Shetah was a last survivor, a last survivor of the pharisaic/rabbinic group. He, too, stood alone between pharisaic/rabbinic Judaism and extinction. He too prevailed.

But for Elijah, the faith in the one universal God and His covenant with Israel might have ended. But for Simeon the Pharisaic/Rabbinic episode might have ended. Simeon was not among the founders of Rabbinic Judaism. He was many generations removed from its inception. He was two generations removed from the peak of its influence. And yet he lived at a time when it might have been snuffed out had it not been for what he was and what he did.

When Simeon came upon the scene, the Second Jewish Commonwealth had won its struggle for independence a century earlier [165 BCE] and had established a monarchy by the year 140 BCE. Three hundred years had passed since the completion of the construction of the Second Temple. Not only that, but by this time its leaders had been transformed from warrior priests to kings who had become powerful, worldly and ambitious.

During his lifetime, the two kings John Hyrcanus and Alexander Jannai had extended the boundaries of Judea from a small ministate around Jerusalem in the fourth pre-Christian century to a kingdom that rivaled King David's Empire. It extended from the Syrian frontier near Damascus to the Sinai Peninsula, including what is now Jordan. They were triumphalist rulers. They had forcibly converted the Idumeans to Judaism. Antipater the Idumean had become a vassal of the court and his son Herod was educated in Rome and ultimately became king.

These kings saw a close link between state power and the power of the priesthood. The priesthood was basically Sadducean. It was opposed to the Pharisee/Rabbinic/Sages whose emphasis was on the Oral Law as the valid interpreter of the written law, and who had already learned from the experience of the cataclysmic days at the end of the First Commonwealth that a technique of survival beyond State and Temple had to be found.

Religious leadership seesawed between Pharisee and Sadducee with both parties in an uneasy balance in the Sanhedrin which by this time had come to represent the religious high court. When Alexander Jannai made his bid to combine the Kingship with the High Priesthood, the Pharisees resisted. The rank and file of the people followed him.

On the Festival of Sukkot [Tabernacles], one of the three Pilgrim Festivals, while the people gathered in their tens of thousands in the Temple grounds with lulav and etrog [palm and citron] in their hands as custom demanded, the king made a move to enter the Holy of Holies to function as High Priest. The Talmud relates that the people hurled their citrons at the king, driving him off the platform. In anger and humiliation, he ordered a massacre of the pharisaic leaders. The leadership in the Sanhedrin passed to the Sadducees; only Simeon was left to represent the Pharisaic point of view, and he too had to flee for his life.

It is interesting to speculate that had the pharisaic exclusion continued, all that we know as Rabbinic Judaism and early Christianity could not have come into being. It is hardly any wonder that Simeon ben Shetah can be perceived as the one who responded to the challenge in such a way as to make the future possible. He becomes a member of that Hall of Fame reserved for "but-for-whoms."

We shall now see how these crucial events are reflected in the Talmud. Let us remember that the Talmud was not designed as a book of history, but as a record of the discussion and elucidation of the Oral Law as codified in the Mishnah and discussed in the academies of the Sages, developing the process of Jewish Law.

The notes of these sessions are the basis of these conclusions. But the obiter dicta, the side remarks of the Sages, the anecdotes they would append in the course of their discussions, become crucial and significant sources of information. They are not in any special order, nor do they follow any special system. But taken together from their very random locations, they yield their crucial secrets. By piecing together random passages such as these, a pattern of meaning emerges clearly. This indeed is the method by which rabbinic texts, properly examined and understood, can yield their secrets.

The Talmudic passage that vividly describes the breach between the Pharisees and the Maccabean kings is introduced in the Tractate Kiddushin, a tractate dealing with the laws of marriage and the strict hereditary requirements in connection with the High Priesthood. One important Oral Law espoused by the Pharisees had to do with the fact that if a woman had been a prisoner of war, her son could never be a High Priest because of this blemish in the ancestry. This the Pharisees invoked against King Alexander Jannai's claim. Here is how it is introduced:

> Abaye also said: Whence do I know it? [i.e. the question of ineligibility] Because it was taught. It once happened that King Jannai went to Kohalith in the wilderness and conquered sixty towns there. On his return he rejoiced exceedingly and invited all the Sages of Israel [to join him in the celebration of victory]. Now there was a man there, frivolous, evil hearted and worthless, named Eliezer ben Poirah [a Sadduccee] who said to King Jannai, "O King Jannai, the hearts of the Pharisees are against

you." [He knew they opposed the King's claim to high priesthood because his mother had been a prisoner of war.] "Then what shall I do?" "Test them by the plate between your eyes." [i.e. claim the high priesthood by putting on the high priestly headgear.] So he tested them by the plate between his eyes. Now an elder named Judah ben Gedidiah [a Pharisee] was present there. "O King Jannai, let the royal crown satisfy you and leave the priestly crown to the seed of Aaron. . . ." The Sages of Israel departed in anger. [cf. Supplement: Simeon ben Shetah #11]

The King turns to ben Poirah and says: "What shall I do?" The answer came quickly: "If you will take my advice, trample them down." The King did just that and ordered a massacre of the Sages, and the narrative concludes:

> Straightway the evil burst forth . . . and all the sages of Israel were massacred and the world was desolate until Simeon ben Shetah came and restored the Torah to its pristine glory. [cf. ibid.]

Thus Simeon ben Shetah, the last surviving member of the Pharisaic party, must flee for his life. But even as a fugitive, the last surviving member of the Pharisaic group, the King cannot get along without him. Two passages, one in the Talmud and one in the Midrash, testify to this. They serve, also, as another example of how crucial historical events emerge from passing references in passages which have primarily an halakhic purpose.

In the tractate Berakhot of the Babylonian Talmud, which deals primarily with the structure of prayer, its time, place and content, there is a detailed discussion on grace after meals, how much one must have eaten, and what prayers must be said. It is in this context that an incident is introduced that reflects the tension between Pharisee and King. Here is the passage in Berakhot:

King Jannai and his queen were taking a meal together.
Now after he had put the Rabbis to death, there was
none to say grace for them. He said to his spouse: I wish
we had someone to say grace for us. She said to him:
Swear to me that if I bring you one you will not harm
him. He swore to her and she brought Simeon ben
Shetah her brother. She placed him between her husband and herself, saying: See what honor I pay you? He
replied: It is not you who honor me. It is the Torah
which honors me. Jannai said to her: You see that he
does not acknowledge my authority! [cf. Supplement:
Simeon ben Shetah #1]

All the elements are here: the massacre of the Pharisees, the
tension of authority between Pharisee and king, and the protec-
tive role of the queen.

But the essence of this passage is halakhic. The king asks
Simeon to say grace. Simeon ironically retorts that he cannot do
this because he has not yet eaten. Food is offered, he eats and
then does the king's bidding. The text proceeds to inform us that
Rabbi Hiyya bar Abba said in the name of Rabbi Johanan that a
man cannot say grace on behalf of others until he has eaten an
amount of food at least the size of an olive with them. A series of
sages examine in detail the minimum that may be eaten before
grace is said, and finally the opinion of another sage is cited, who
states: "Moses instituted for Israel the benediction [for saying
grace] at the time when the manna descended for them."

But for us it is the incidental episode that precedes this
discussion that captures our interest. For it provides us with
added crucial information about Simeon and his role.

We encounter a discussion on the same theme of the saying
of grace that involves the participation of Simeon in the same
banquet, but with some additional details. This is the account in
Genesis Rabbah, a collection of rabbinic homilies commenting
on the Torah text that appeared approximately the same time as
the Babylonian Talmud. It will prove very instructive to take a
good look at it and then compare it with the passage from
Berakhot:

Rabbi Jeremiah asked: Can Grace be recited in common
by including one who dined on vegetables? [The question may be answered by the following incident] Three
hundred nazirites came up in the days of Simeon ben
Shetah. For one hundred and fifty he found grounds for
absolution, but for the other hundred and fifty he could
find no grounds. Accordingly he repaired to King Jannai and said to him: "Three hundred nazirites have
come up and they need nine hundred sacrifices. Do you
give half and I will give half." Jannai did so, but a
talebearer went and informed him that Simeon had
given nothing. When Simeon learned this he fled. Some
time after certain Persian dignitaries were dining at King
Jannai's table, and they observed: "We remember that
there used to be an old man here who spoke to us words
of wisdom." [Jannai] said to his sister: "Send for him to
come here." "Give him your promise of safety," she replied "and he will come." The promise having been
given, he sat between the King and Queen. "Why did you
fool me?" asked the King. "Heaven forfend!" [he re-
plied] "I did not fool you, but you gave of yours [money],
while I gave of mine [knowledge]!" [cf. Supplement: Simeon ben Shetah #4]

This, in the middle of a long and detailed discussion about
how and when grace after meals must be recited.

If we compare this passage with the passage from Berakhot,
we see clearly that we are talking about traditions of the same
banquet, and the same summoning of Simeon. The first passage
gives no details about what the banquet was about, and is at pains
to make reference to the massacre of Pharisees and the flight of
Simeon. The second passage informs us that the guests of honor
consisted of a Persian diplomatic visit, who specifically asked for
Simeon and embarrassed the King into inviting him.

Here the reason given for the tension is a different one. It
has to do with the absolution of nazirites from their vows, either
by finding legal grounds for their absolution, or bringing a variety of birds for sacrifice. Simeon provides the legal absolution,

while he gets the King to pay. An informer tells the king he has been fooled by Simeon and Simeon flees.

One should note the role of the informer, which we already encountered in the first passage we dealt with in this lecture. There the informer is named: Eliezer ben Poirah. Here, he is anonymous.

Let us see what we can understand from this nazirite episode. The *nazir* is described in detail in Numbers 6. To be a *nazir* is to take a vow of consecration to the service of God, renouncing the use of wine and cutting off one's hair. Such a vow can only be annulled by a special sacrifice in the Temple, by the absolution of a priest, or by the intervention of father or husband in the case of a daughter or a wife.

The power to find ways of absolution was vested in the priesthood, but one of the ways in which the Pharisees challenged their authority was to assume that power themselves, using the Oral Law as their basis for absolution. So in this instance, Jannai, who claims High Priesthood, is trapped into paying for the sacrifices of half the nazirites, while Simeon boldly asserts the authority which the Pharisees are taking over from the priesthood!

The two variant passages about the banquet and the grace ritual are very instructive in how Talmudic passages can be used to extrapolate historical realities. In each instance, the discussions about the traditions of the rituals around grace before meals are basically the same. What varies are the accounts of why Simeon was in flight, how he came to the banquet, and his tension with the King. Together the two accounts flesh out the details of the event.

However, what emerges clearly, despite the variant traditions, were the basic facts that there was a serious tension between the King and Pharisees; that Simeon is the leading spokesman and activist for the pharisaic side; that the breach involved a massacre, according to one tradition, whereas in the other tradition the massacre is not mentioned. The tradition that speaks about the massacre is vague about the nature of the banquet and suggests no reason for the breach. The tradition which introduces the state visit of Persian dignitaries locates a

reason for the breach in the question of the absolution of nazirite vows.

Furthermore, the first passage we examined, the one that
names the Sadducaic informer, ben Poirah, sees the reason in the
Pharisaic refusal to accept the validity of Jannai's claim for the
High Priesthood. What we can be reasonably certain, in the context of these passages, is that together they flesh out the picture
of this tension and of Simeon's central role in it.

The issue surfaces on another occasion over Pharisaic insis-
tence that the King is not above the law. Again the Pharisaic
position on this comes out in incidental fashion, in the Tractate
Sanhedrin of the Babylonian Talmud, folio 19a. Here the discussion centers around an interesting law that whereas Kings of the
Davidic Dynasty may judge and be judged, Kings of Israel may
neither judge nor be judged.

The exception with respect to the Kings of Israel in the
discussion immediately seems to call for an explanation:

> But why is this prohibition of the Kings of Israel? Be-
> cause of an instance which happened with a slave of
> King Jannai who killed a man. Simeon ben Shetah said
> to the Sages: "Set your eyes boldly upon him and let us
> judge him." So they sent the King word saying: "Your
> slave has killed a man." Thereupon he sent him [the
> slave] to be tried. But they again sent him a message:
> "You too must come here." The king accordingly came
> and sat down. Then Simeon ben Shetah said: "Stand on
> your feet, King Jannai, and let the witnesses testify
> against you; yet it is not before us that you stand, but
> before him who spoke and the world came into being."
> "I shall not act in accordance with what you say, but in
> accordance with what your colleagues say," he an-
> swered. Simeon then turned to the right and to the left,
> but they all [for fear of the King] looked down at the
> ground. [cf. Supplement, Simeon ben Shetah #5]

From this passage Simeon ben Shetah very clearly emerges
as one of those incredible "but-for-whoms," a lone Pharisee in a

High Court dominated by Sadducaic stooges, firmly standing his ground. He calls on God to bring the craven to account, and we are informed that "Gabriel came and smote them to the ground and they died." It was then enacted, we learn from this text, that a king not of the House of David may neither judge nor be judged. It looks like a victory for the king. It reflects the fury of the king directed at his Pharisaic opponents. But the setback was temporary, for Simeon had stood his ground. His own persistence had made the long range triumph possible. The improbable miracles notwithstanding, that fact shines clearly through the text.

Thus far for written hints. What about evidence from silence? Here too we can find evidence for the deep and bitter split between Pharisee and King.

In the Babylonian Talmud Tractate Shabbath, which deals in the fullest detail with the laws of the Sabbath and how it is to be observed, there is a detailed discussion about the kindling of the Sabbath lights. A discussion follows with respect to what oil and wicks may be used, where the lights are to be placed, and many other such details.

Since the subject of discussion is the kindling of lights, someone introduces the subject of Hanukkah lights. Abruptly in the middle of the discussion, we read the following:

What is [the reason of] Hanukkah? For our rabbis taught: On the twenty-fifth of Kislev [commence] the days of Hanukkah which are eight on which lamentation for the dead and fasting are forbidden. For when the Greeks entered the Temple they defiled all the oils therein and when the Hasmonean dynasty prevailed against and defeated them, they made search and found only one cruse of oil which lay with the seal of the High Priest, but which contained sufficient for one day's lighting, yet a miracle was wrought therein and they lit [the lamp] therewith for eight days. The following year these days were appointed a Festival with [the recital] of Hallel and Thanksgiving. [cf. Supplement, Simeon ben Shetah #2]

Why at this stage does one have to be asked "Why Hanuk-kah?" Was not the achievement of freedom and the establish-ment of the Hasmonean Dynasty not an unforgettable event? Did one have to ask: "Why Passover?" or "Why Shabbat?" Did not every Jew know the answer to that? And here the reason seems to have been forgotten and the Hasmoneans are men-tioned as with the flick of a wrist!

It is clear that what has happened, in effect, is that with the ultimate triumph of the Pharisees, and their hand firmly at the rudder of the ship of the development of Judaism, a rewriting of history takes place, and the Hasmoneans are practically written out of it. You see the evidence in the canonization of the Hebrew Bible, which deliberately omits including the Apocrypha, princi-pally because they contain the Books of the Maccabees. It is the Christian Church, by its inclusion of these books, that rescued the detailed history of the Maccabees for us.

Now we can see more clearly the depth of the schism, and how vividly and poignantly it emerges from the Rabbinic texts we have examined.

Is Simeon, then, all combat struggle and tension? Is there no softness to him? Here are some texts that show his gentler side. In the Midrash Deuteronomy Rabbah [iii:3] we read the following:

It is related of Simeon ben Shetah that he once bought an ass from an Arab. His disciple came and found a precious stone suspended from its neck. They said to him: *It is the blessing of the Lord that enriches.* [Prov. 10:22] Rabbi Simeon ben Shetah replied: "I have purchased an ass, but I have not purchased a precious stone." He then went and returned it to the Arab and the latter exclaimed to him: "Blessed be the Lord God of Simeon ben Shetah." [cf. Supplement: Simeon ben Shetah #6]

Here we see a man of integrity and of compassion. It is an example of Jewish-Arab relations that we could well use in our own time if only we could break through the barriers of passion and understanding.

Simeon differed sharply with his colleague Judah ben Tabbai over the issue of capital punishment. As a result of that difference it was Simeon's position that to achieve a conviction for capital punishment, it was necessary to have two eyewitnesses who had not only seen the crime performed but had also warned the perpetrator against the consequence of the act. As a result of this, capital punishment was practically never carried out.

Another example of his compassion and sense of justice: In marriage, the woman's rights were contained in the ketubah, the marriage contract, but up to this time it was not in her possession. Thus she could not readily produce evidence of her rights. We learn this, interestingly, from another of those fascinating Talmudic asides. A series of Rabbinic rulings are being listed in the Tractate Shabbat 14b:

> For, it was taught, Jose ben Joezer of Zereda and Jose ben Johanan of Jerusalem decreed uncleanness in respect to heathens and glassware, Simeon ben Shetah instituted the woman's marriage settlement, and imposed uncleanness upon metal utensils. [Supplement: Simeon ben Shetah #7]

When we add to this the fact that he instituted the compulsory education of children—so far ahead of his time—we see the quality of this extraordinary man "but-for-whom."

Gradually, as we examine the process of the development of Rabbinic-Pharisaic Judaism, through its system of hermeneutic and interpretation, through its system of Midrash, we shall see how this process, at every level, is a form of *derashah*, a sermon process at its highest and most effective level to shape Judaism for its survival.

Simeon prevented the process from being destroyed.

Chapter Four

Hillel

We have already met Simeon ben Shetah, the man who rescued Rabbinic Judaism from extinction.

Now we meet our second giant, Hillel. Hillel may be described as the "Euclid" of Midrash, the man who created the logical structure that made it something more than ad hoc exegesis. *Midrash* was already in existence. It was already in being during the time of Ezra, and perhaps earlier, as a technique of linking the Oral Law to the Written Law, and of interpreting Torah to the people. But it existed as a natural, unstructured, un-self-conscious method. Hillel gave it form and substance. He shaped a system, and the system, later expanded, shaped the process. Whether he invented the method, or whether he borrowed it from the Greeks, is a matter of debate among scholars.

What made the difference? The appearance on the scene of Alexander the Great, and his thrust into Egypt and the Middle East, was the decisive event. By the third pre-Christian century, and a full century after Ezra, Greek culture and the culture of the Middle East encountered each other and influenced each other. Each made the other define itself more precisely.

This after all was the age of the culmination of Greek philosophy, with Aristotle, Alexander's mentor, as the intellectual leader. Greek culture tended to be linear, and logically precise thanks to the work of Socrates, Plato, Aristotle and the Stoa. Rabbinic Judaism appeared to be non-systematic, stream-of-consciousness in style. The Rabbinic dictum was: *"Ein mukdam um'uhar baTorah."* ["There is no before or after in Torah."] You could put Moses at the feet of Akiba a thousand years later, with no contradiction. One might say that the closest to this thought system in our time might be found in the works of James Joyce, especially in his *Ulysses*.

The interpenetration of these two worlds of thought influenced each other. So there are some who think that Hillel applied the Greek techniques of logic to the Rabbinic method of exegesis. The Talmudic tradition is very clear on this:

> Hillel the Elder expounded seven exegetical rules in the presence of the Sons of Bathyra, viz. the inference drawn from a minor premise to a major, the inference drawn from a similarity of words or phrases. . . . These are the seven rules which Hillel the Elder expounded in the presence of the Sons of Bathyra. [cf. Supplement: Hillel #4]

This is what you read in *Avot d'Rabbi Nathan* of the Babylonian Talmud. It is well to bear this passage in mind for subsequent consideration, especially the reference to the Bnai Bathyra.

These seven rules of Hillel, later expanded to thirteen, became the fixed and formalized basis of the hermeneutic of the Rabbinic Schools, which ultimately shaped the Mishnah and the Talmud.

Let us see precisely what these seven rules were:

(1) The inference drawn from a minor premise to a major.
(2) The inference drawn from a similarity of words and phrases.
(3) A general principle established on the basis of a law contained in one verse or of laws contained in two verses.
(4) The rule when a generalization is followed in the text by a specification.
(5) The rule when a specification is followed in the text by a generalization.
(6) The inference drawn from an analogous passage elsewhere.
(7) The interpretation of a word or passage from its context.

This then is Hillel, architect of Rabbinic exegesis, Father of Midrash. He was to Midrash what Euclid was to geometry!

He was more than that. He was also the founder of a dynasty of Rabbinic Sages who occupy the role of Patriarch, that is, titular head of the Rabbinic Jewish process. His descendants continued in this role until the fourth century, in Judea, until the Patriarchate was ended by the growing power of the Byzantine Church, and the center of Judaism shifted finally from Judea to Babylonia.

In fact this role was perceived as so important that Talmudic tradition has it that Hillel was descended from King David. This was a way of saying that the Davidic Dynasty did not end with the destruction of the First Jewish State, but was in fact reconstituted through Hillel. It had a Messianic overtone, subtly counterposed to the early Christian claims for the same crown!

Thirdly, Hillel may well have been a contemporary of Jesus. Here is what we read in the Tractate Shabbat of the Talmud:

> Surely it was taught: Hillel and Simeon [his son], Gamaliel and Simeon wielded their Patriarchate during one hundred years of the Temple's existence. . . . [cf. Supplement: Hillel #3]

We know, of course, that the Temple was destroyed in the year 70. That means that Hillel became Patriarch in the year 30 BCE or thereabouts. Many scholars place the birth of Jesus at 3 BCE. On that assumption, and giving Hillel forty years' tenure, it is quite possible that Jesus, at the age of twelve or thirteen, had studied with him. [Jewish boys began studying Torah at the age of five or six.] Remember Simeon ben Shetah's innovation? Perhaps he even heard his answer to the pagan who asked to be taught Judaism on one foot: *"Ma d'alakh sanay l'havrakh lo ta'aved."* ["Do not unto others that which is hateful to thee."]

Simeon ben Shetah and Hillel were separated from each other by three quarters of a century. The changes in the interim were enormous, and a swift look at the historical development of the period will be useful. Simeon appeared on the scene at the height of Jewish independence that followed the Maccabean Revolt. Rome was in the background as an ally.

By Hillel's time that situation had changed radically. The later Maccabean kings squandered their power and their coun-

try's independence, and by 42 BCE Pompey occupied Judea, and
from that time on until the War with Rome, the Jewish state was
an occupied and vassal country.

The glory days of the Pharisaic/Rabbinic return to power and
influence came after the death of Alexander Jannai and during
the reign of his Queen, Salome Alexandra, Simeon ben Shetah's
sister. We recall how Salome negotiated the reconciliation between Simeon and the King. When she assumed full power, she
encouraged Simeon's assumption of full power for the Pharisee/
Sages, unseating the priestly-kingly oriented Sadducees.

After Salome's death, inter dynastic struggles caused up-
heavals in the Maccabean royal household. The struggle between the brothers John Hyrcanus II and Aristobulus brought
on the direct intervention of Rome through Pompey who in-
stalled full Roman military power by 42 BCE. Pompey showed
his power by entering the Temple and desecrating it. In a sense it
was the Hellenistic Maccabean struggle all over again. During
the siege of the Temple Area, Ptolemy had desecrated it by cata-
pulting a swine's head into the Temple area.

This was reflected in the generation of Hillel's teachers,
Shemaiah and Abtalion, who counseled the sages of their time to
keep their distance from political power. It was also expressed in
their dictum of Shemaiah: "Love work and hate mastery, and
make yourself not known to the government!" [Pirke Avot 1:10]
and also in the dictum: "Cursed be he who teaches his son
Greek!" [B. Sotah 49a]

The turn was inward, and its emphasis once again on exegesis of Torah, to which Hillel had committed himself, and in
which he excelled. It is during this period that the gains of Simeon ben Shetah were eroded, and it almost seemed that the
Rabbinic enterprise was back to square one. The Sons of Bathyra
had become the intellectual and spiritual leaders, and presumably knew little of the Oral Law. From what we know of them,
they may have been Sadducaic in their leanings.

This is where Hillel comes in. Again, we get this crucial
information by indirection, as we did in the case of Simeon ben
Shetah. In this case it is a question of the Passover, and how it can
be proved that the sacrifice of the paschal lamb must be per-

formed even if the Passover occurs on the eve of the Sabbath when all work is prohibited.

It is in this context that Hillel enters the scene. We read in the Talmud *Pesahim* [66a]:

> Our Rabbis taught: This halakhah was forgotten by the B'nei Bathyra. On one occasion the fourteenth of Nisan fell on the Sabbath and they forgot and did not know whether the Passover overrides the Sabbath or not. Said they, "Is there any man who knows whether the Passover overrides the Sabbath or not?" They were told: "There is a certain man who has come up from Babylonia, Hillel the Babylonian by name, who served two of the greatest men of the time, and he knows whether the Passover overrides the Sabbath or not." Thereupon they summoned him and said to him, "Do you know whether the Passover overrides the Sabbath or not?" [cf. Supplement: Hillel #6]

In characteristic Jewish fashion, Hillel, who suddenly comes upon the scene as though from nowhere, answers a question with a question!

> "Have we then only one Passover during the year which overrides the Sabbath?" replied he to them. "Surely we have many more than two hundred Passovers during the year which override the Sabbath!" Said they to him: "How do you know it?" He answered them: " 'In its appointed time' is stated in connection with the Passover, and 'In its appointed time' is stated in connection with the *tamid*. Just as 'In its appointed time' which is said in connection with the *tamid* overrides the Sabbath, so 'In its appointed time,' which is said in connection with the Passover, overrides the Sabbath. Moreover, it follows, *a minori,* if the *tamid*, the omission of which is not punished by *kareth* [death penalty], overrides the Sabbath, then the Passover, the neglect of which *is* punished by *kareth*, is it not logical that it overrides the

Sabbath!" They immediately set him at their head and appointed him *Nasi* [ibid.]

This passage has been quoted at length because it is another crucial example of how casually the sages record such a vital and central development. The Hillel, about whom we learn in another place that he instituted the seven rules of exegesis, is here described as applying those rules to solve a problem nobody else could handle.

The fact that the B'nei Bathyra are described as having forgotten the *halakhah,* and that there was no one around who appeared to know, indicates an apparent takeover in Judea by non-rabbinic forces when a problem that needs to be solved crops up. Whether you were guided by the Sages or those of Sadducaic influence, whether you accepted or rejected the Oral Law, Passover had to be observed, the paschal lamb had to be prepared, and, here, along comes Passover on a Sabbath eve, and with it the conflict that needs to be resolved.

What does Hillel do? He uses two of his exegetical rules to show why the paschal lamb must be prepared even on the Sabbath, despite the prohibition against work for that day.

He first makes use of Principle Number Two, the inference drawn from a similarity of words and phrases in different places in the text. The phrase "in its time" [*b'mo'ado*] is used in connection with the Tamid offering which is to be made twice a day, including the Sabbath, where four lambs instead of two as on other days are offered up. [Num. 28:1ff]

Now since that phrase "in its time" [*b'mo'ado*] is also used in connection with the paschal offering, you may deduce that it can be done on the Sabbath even if the Sabbath is not specifically indicated.

He then uses a second exegetical method to arrive at the same result. This time he uses Principle One, the inference drawn from a minor premise to a major premise. He notes that the non-performance of the paschal sacrifice is punishable by death [karet], whereas the non-performance of the Tamid is punishable by a sin offering.

Now, if a sacrifice, the omission of which is punishable by a less severe penalty, must nevertheless be performed on the Sabbath, does it not stand to reason that the Passover offering must be given on the Sabbath when its appointed time comes on the Sabbath? For even though its performance on the Sabbath is not specified since a death penalty is incurred for non-performance, and the appointed time is clearly stated, the answer is clear.

One should note that Hillel uses not one but two exegetical routes, both of which arrive at the same conclusion. It was really a "fail-safe" approach to exegesis that was at the basis of the Rabbinic Jewish process, that did not take lightly the exegetical process, as it did not take lightly the relationship of the Oral Law to the Written Law. It is no wonder that the people concluded that Hillel was their man.

Nevertheless, they do not let him off the hook. When he thinks he has neatly solved the problem, they hurl another question at him. He has done well thus far. He has proven by the intersection of two of his seven exegetical methods that the Passover Sacrifice could be performed on the Sabbath. So far so good. Now comes the question designed to stump him. For we learn:

> [After his appointment as *Nasi*] he was sitting and lecturing the whole day on the laws of Passover. He began rebuking them with words. Said he to them: "What caused it for you that I should come up from Babylonia to be a *Nasi* over you? It was your indolence . . . " [ibid.]

That was the point at which the people decided that he whom they had raised so high needed to be brought down a peg or two. So they said to him:

> "Master, what if a man forgot and did not bring a knife on the eve of the Sabbath?" "I have heard this law," he answered, "but have forgotten it." [ibid.]

The great scholar, who seemed capable of remembering what everybody else had forgotten, was now pleading ignorance. Was he now to be banished with the B'nei Bathyra? Not exactly. For he quickly continued:

> "But leave it to Israel: if they are not prophets, they are the children of prophets!" On the morrow, he whose Passover was a lamb stuck it [the knife] in its wool; he whose Passover was a goat stuck it between its horns. He saw the incident and recollected the *halakhah* and said: "Thus have I received the tradition from my teachers." [ibid.]

It should be noted how folk memory or custom, things done by the people without their quite remembering why, was included with exegesis as an equally important way of determining what the Torah was really about.

The almost casual, off-hand way in which such very important statements are made about logical, philosophical and theological aspects of the development of Judaism should not escape our attention. Law and custom are very closely intertwined and interrelated here, as in Roman Law, for example, and it is Hillel who brings this fact sharply into focus.

What manner of man was this Hillel? Here and there in the Talmud we have bits of information, which, put together, gives us the image of a gentle, sensitive, patient, peace-loving individual who made a profound impact on folk memory.

Hillel came from Babylonia. He was part of that great diaspora community that came into being after the destruction of the First Temple. He came from that Babylonia which Jeremiah had urged to "dig in" for the long pull. He came from that Babylonia that was to become the great and creative center of world Judaism after the Second Commonwealth finally came to an end.

As a young man, and already married, he was a struggling scholar with a hunger for learning. His brother Shebna chose the course of making a fortune. Hillel chose the path of study. When he was on his way to success, Shebna said to him: "Let us become partners and divide the profit." [B. Sotah 21a] By then it was too late, and he received a stinging rejection. Had he funded the education of his brother, like the brother of Maimonides, who did just that for his brilliant and gifted brother, it might have been otherwise.

Hillel did it the hard way. He made his way to Jerusalem, to study in the academy of Shemaiah and Abtalion where he attempted to support his family and study at the same time. He was the image of the struggling and starving seminarian. It was related that he had some part-time job and earned one *tropaik* per diem. He used half to feed his family, and half to pay the tuition for the daily lectures. This little fact indicates how the academies were structured. Presumably the teachers had to live too!

Here is how the Talmud reports the episode:

> One day he found nothing to earn, and the guard at the House of Learning would not permit him to enter. He climbed up and sat upon the window, to hear the words of the living God from Shemaiah and Abtalion. They say that it was the eve of the Sabbath of the winter solstice and snow fell down upon him from heaven. When the dawn rose, Shemaiah said to Abtalion: Brother Abtalion, on every day this house is light and today it is dark. Is it perhaps a cloudy day? They looked up and saw the figure of a man in the window. They went up and found him covered by three cubits of snow. They removed him, bathed and anointed him and placed him opposite the fire and they said: This man deserves that the Sabbath be profaned on his behalf. [Supplement: Hillel #2]

Now that is an eager student for you! This hunger for learning was a benchmark of rabbinic values that has endured through the generations of time. So impressive was this fact that the story is told in connection with a Talmudic thesis, that whether you are poor, rich or pleasure loving, it is no excuse not to study Torah. In fact, when a poor man dies and claims entry to heaven, and when asked why he did not study Torah, he replies that he was too poor, he is abruptly told: "Were you as poor as Hillel, who was not deterred by being poor?" At which point the story is told, and the poor man who would not study Torah is turned aside!

Shemaiah and Abtalion were Hillel's teachers. Tradition has it that both were converts to Judaism, descended from Sisera, the Canaanite warrior, whom Deborah, that great feminist of the period of the Judges, had defeated. They were an important link in the chain of Torah study. They were among the *zugot* [pairs] who are listed in the first chapter of *Pirkei Avot* as a link between the Men of the Great Synagogue and the rabbinic sages. They taught, as has already been indicated, during the period of oppression at the time of Ptolemy's occupation of Judea [circa 40 BCE]. It is likely that the Polion mentioned by Josephus [Ant. XV:1] in his account of the Pharisees was Abtalion.

It may be concluded that Hillel's very patient and liberal attitude toward converts to Judaism may well have stemmed from this tradition. This openness to proselytes, not in the high handed method of conversion or that which was practiced by John Hyrcanus [and by forces in triumphant Islam and Christianity, for that matter] but in the gentle persuasive humane way of Hillel, is another quality about him that stands out.

There were some great eras of proselytization in Jewish history. The period from the end of the Judges to the establishment of the Davidic and Solomonic monarchy was one. The surviving Canaanites were not eliminated. They became Jews. Then we had the period of the second pre-Christian century when many Phoenecians in the Roman Empire became Jews, after their defeat in the Punic Wars. There was also the period of Maccabean triumphalism.

The pagan who came to Shammai with the proposal that he would accept Judaism if Shammai could teach it to him while he stood on one foot was greeted with sharp and contemptuous rejection. Shammai drove the man away in anger. Not so Hillel. In fact the pagan took great pains to irritate Hillel. He picked his bath time to come storming into the house claiming a great emergency. When Hillel would emerge he would ask him a foolish question. To these questions Hillel unflappably gave patient answers.

A sample: "Why are the heads of Babylonians round?" or

"Why are the eyes of the Palmyrians bleared?" or "Why are the feet of the Africans wide?" He had made a wager that he could force Hillel to lose his temper. Hillel, each time, dripping wet and wrapped in his towel, would gently say, "You ask an important question," and then give him the answer.

Making a final effort the pagan blurted out: "May there be none like you. You made me lose my wager that I could make you lose your temper."

To which Hillel replied: "Better you lose your wager, than I my temper." At this point the pagan offered to adopt Judaism if Hillel could teach it to him while he stood on one foot. He hoped that on a question so close to Hillel's heart, he might provoke him to a Shammai-type response. Instead he received this reply: "Do not do unto others that which is hateful to thee. That is the Torah, the rest is commentary. Go and study it!"

Recalling how he upbraided his fellow Jews over their neglect of the Torah, when he first became *Nasi*, his gentleness to the pagan stands out. It is, one may suppose, a natural tendency for us to be harder on those closer to us.

To his gentleness we can add humility and a profound concern for his fellow man. When his wife gave away his dinner to a poor man who came to their door, he praised her highly instead of upbraiding her for not having his dinner on the table on time! When an acquaintance of his who had once been wealthy lost his fortune, Hillel helped him keep up appearances by procuring a horse for him to ride upon and a servant to run before him. When, one day, the servant failed to appear, Hillel himself took his place and ran ahead of the horse for three miles. This was not only an act of great kindness. It was also an early reference to jogging!

He extended the definition of religious duty. One day on his way to the bath, his disciples asked: "Where are you going?" To which he replied: "To do a religious duty." "Your bath a religious duty?" they replied incredulously. "Yes," he replied:

> "if the statues of kings, which are erected in theatres and circuses, are scoured and washed by the man who is appointed to look after them, and who thereby obtains

his maintenance through them—nay more, he is ex-
alted in the company of the great of the kingdom—how
much more I, who have been created in the Image and
Likeness of God!" [Supplement: Hillel #9]

And in another version of the same thing, in reply to that
question: "Where are you going?" his answer was, "To do a chari-
table deed for a guest in my house." They then asked whether
this guest stayed with him every day, to which he replied: "This
poor soul—is it not a guest in the body, here today and gone
tomorrow?" Body and soul in the service of the divine was at the
core of his being and of his thought.

Humility and study of Torah lay at the core of his conviction, as this passage from the Ethics of the Fathers [Pirke Avot]
testifies:

He who magnifies his name, destroys it, and he who
does not study deserves to die; and he who makes
worldly use of the crown of Torah shall waste away.
[Pirkei Avot 1:13]

His deep faith in the principle of reward and punishment is
encapsulated in his comment upon seeing a skull floating down a
river. When I think of this I think of Hamlet's reaction to the
skull held up by the gravedigger: "Alas, poor Yorik, I knew him
well." To Hillel the skull represented Everyman, and his comment was:

"Because you drowned some one, you were drowned,
and the end of those who drowned you will be that you
will be drowned." [ibid. 2:6]

Hamlet may have known poor Yorik well; Hillel knew the
moral basis of Everyman's destiny even better.

Finally, it is simply impossible to speak of Hillel without
including Shammai. We have already indicated that Hillel estab-
lishes a "dynasty" in the development of Rabbinic Judaism, the
Hillelite dynasty that dominated it for almost four hundred

years. But in his own time, while this is being shaped, he was one of a pair, the last of the pairs, or *zugot* as they are known.

The chain of tradition, as we have it in the *Pirkei Avot,* goes from Moses to Joshua to the prophets to the Men of the Great Synagogue, to Simon the Just [third century BCE], the last of the Men of the Great Synagogue, who is followed by Antigonos of Socho. Then follow the pairs.

It should be noted that Antigonos is the only sage in the series with a Greek name, and this probably reflects the high degree of assimilation during the period immediately preceding the Maccabean Revolution.

The pairs, and their special dicta, are then listed: Jose ben Joezer and Jose ben Johanan; Joshua ben Perahia and Nitai of Arbel; Judah ben Tabbai and Simeon ben Shetah; Shemaiah and Abtalion; and finally, Hillel and Shammai. After that Pirkei Avot lists individual sages.

Hillel and Shammai differed sharply in temperament and approach. Their rulings on Halakhah were usually quite different, and this debate continued on through their Schools, with the School of Hillel usually differing, in interpretations, from the School of Shammai. Usually, because the Hillelites won control, the decisions were decided in favor of the Hillelites.

The Talmud reflects this victory. The portrait of Hillel and Shammai we get in the Talmud is filtered through a Hillelite prism. Hillel is gentle and patient; Shammai is irascible and severe. Hillel is a moderate; Shammai an extremist.

We ought, however, not permit ourselves to be influenced too much in this direction, much as we are tempted to like and to admire Hillel. For the reality is that the Talmud developed along dialectic lines. In other religious cultures as they developed, dissent was suppressed, and only one view and one conclusion preserved. Not so in the Talmud. All sides of arguments are presented. All sides are preserved. When a ruling is finally made with the term, "and the sages say," it makes a statement about the consensus ruling, but does not obliterate the minority view.

How this works can be seen in two conflicting *midrashim* on the same event. With respect to the Revelation at Mount Sinai, we have one *midrash* [which we have already encountered] that describes God as offering the Torah to all the nations of the world, and each turns it down after inquiring what was in it. Only Israel responds: "We will do and we will listen!" [*na'aseh v'nishma*] They accepted it willingly, sight unseen.

But then there is that other *midrash* on the same theme. As the people of Israel stood at the foot of the mountain, watching it in volcanic convulsion as God is about to speak, they are terrified and want to flee. God tears the mountain from its roots, holds it over them like a huge cone, and says: "If you do not accept my Torah, here will be your graves!"

Was the Torah accepted willingly or through coercion? The answer is the dialectic. The answer is both!

In later generations the dialectic argument is between Abaye and Rava. So taken together, the debates between the House of Hillel and the House of Shammai, and Abaye and Rava, and all between, are a fabric of dialectic, varied streams and eddies emptying into the vast Sea of the Talmud.

There are some who think that Shammai represented aspects of the Sadducaic point of view that was incorporated into Rabbinic Judaism as a strategy of internalizing polarization to prevent a destructive splintering process in a crucial moment of historical development. Some believe that Shammai represented the upper classes and aristocracy while Hillel spoke for the common people. Shammai seemed to stand for static, reactionary particularism, while Hillel represented progressive universalism. In exegesis, the Shammaites were concerned with context, while the Hillelites would disregard context. The same word in two different contexts would be enough for Hillel to make an exegetical decision. For the Shammaites, creation was a one time event; for the Hillelites it was a continuing process. It was they who wrote into the prayer book the phrase that God "daily renews the work of creation."

Shammai rejected certain of Hillel's principles. He interpreted Scripture according to the spirit, while Hillel interpreted according to the letter. He would never have accepted his validation of the Paschal sacrifice on the basis of one word [like *b'mo'ado*] in two different contexts.

Hillel and Shammai differed on the principles of cause and

effect. Shammaites saw the effect as a direct link to the cause, that cause and effect were one continuous process. Hillelites tended to reduce causation to mere external succession in time, one thing after another without necessary relationship. In the denial of the principle of causality there is a line from Hillel through Sextus Empiricus, Al Ghazali and Hume!

On the question of divorce, Shammai was stricter. Hillelites extended the number of grounds for divorce.

The Talmud records that for two and a half years the House of Hillel and the House of Shammai debated whether it were better that man had not been created. And after a long debate they came to the conclusion: "It were better that he had not been created; but since he has been created, let him examine his deeds!"

We have seen Hillel as the developer of the exegetic method that is at the basis of the development of the rabbinic hermeneutic that finally resulted in the Talmud. We have examined Hillel as a person, gentle, patient, perceptive, communicating. We have examined Hillel in his role in the dialectic form that is at the basis of the Talmudic process. By his time the process is firmly established. It has developed and gone forward. Jeremiah's advice in the fifth pre-Christian century has been heeded. It has taken form. It not only can withstand the shock of another disaster of military defeat and exile. It is in a position to assume leadership. It is ready for his disciple Johanan ben Zakkai.

Chapter Five

Johanan ben Zakkai

We now meet Johanan ben Zakkai, who took the organized structure of Rabbinic Judaism, now fleshed out and developed, and
made it an effective tool for survival. The time for the testing of
the Rabbinic maxim that "God provides the cure in advance of
the disease" had come. [B. Meg. 13b] Jeremiah's letter to the
exiles had suggested the cure. It was developed during the period of the Second Commonwealth, with its variety and its creativity. Now came the disease, in the days of Johanan.

In his time the Wars with Rome will come to a climax. The
State and Temple will be destroyed. The process of diaspora and
exile, though destined to take several centuries, had begun.

See how a contemporary, Tacitus, describes the event:

> The Jews, their backs to the wall, because of the siege,
> without hope for either peace or surrender, finally be-
> gan to die of hunger. The streets filled up with corpses.
> There was no time to bury the dead. . . . It is related
> that Titus took counsel with his advisors whether or not
> to destroy the Temple. There were many who believed
> that he ought not to do it; that it would be a pity to
> destroy such an eminent shrine. Sparing it would be a
> great tribute to the moderation of Rome. . . . Others,
> however, and Titus was on their side, insisted vigor-
> ously on its destruction, which would result in the utter
> destruction of the religion of the Jews and the Chris-
> tians, who, though hostile to each other, had a common
> origin. The Christians stemmed from the Jews. Hence,
> if you tore up the roots, the whole plant would perish.

[Th. Reinach, Textes d'Auteurs Grecs et Romains, Paris 1895 p. 324]*

And Rabbinic sources record:

A catapult was brought, and a swine's head was set into the catapult and hurled toward the sacrificial lambs of the altar. It was then Jerusalem was captured. Meanwhile Johanan ben Zakkai waited trembling. . . . When Rabban Johanan ben Zakkai heard that Jerusalem was destroyed and the Temple was aflame, he tore his clothing and his disciples tore their clothing, and they wept, crying aloud and mourning. [Abot d'Rabbi Nathan 20a]

But that was not the end, as we well know, because of Johanan ben Zakkai, whom we can characterize as another "but-for-whom." But for him, who knows what might have happened.

These are the crucial years. The Roman noose tightens. Jewish resistance mounts. A sense of the imminence of Messianic times, a sense last felt during the Maccabean Revolt almost two centuries previously, is in the air. Some Messianic claimants are sure the solution will come through war and divine intervention. Other messianic claimants see a spiritual intervention. As has already been noted, the time was at hand for the emergence of the siblings, Rabbinic Judaism and early Christianity.

Hillel, as we have seen, prepared the way. He fixed the basis for the system of exegesis. He began the dialectic system with the Hillel-Shammai debates. He established a line of authority. The shaping of the institutions moved forward. A High Court, known as Bet Din, takes shape, and, at its side, a High Academy, known as Beth Hamidrash.

The appearance of Johanan ben Zakkai marks the beginning of a new era. Jeremiah might have done just that had he survived the turbulence of the Babylonian Wars; and had he not been hijacked to Egypt and ultimately assassinated by extremists. Johanan confronted the extremists of his time and survived sufficiently to make the crucial difference.

Let us recall how we spoke of the crisis of the Roman War

and the Jewish options. Outwardly the struggle was against Rome. Inwardly it was between extremists and moderates on the one hand, and instant messianists and long range messianists on the other. Both military extremists and instant messianists operated within the parameters of the Pharisaic/Rabbinic movement.

Johanan made the choice for moderation against enormous pressures from all sides. He realized that the War against Rome could not be won militarily. He understood that the struggle must be continued in other ways. Therefore he made a non-aggression pact with Rome, to win time to do what must be done for the transition that was coming.

Let us see how this man emerges from the Talmudic record. Let us examine his personality, see what kind of man he was, and then examine precisely what he did and how he did it.

There is a delicate irony about how he emerges from the Talmudic tradition. His role is described with subtlety, with irony, and a touch of understatement.

Note how it is done. This tradition is found thrice, once in the Tractate Sukka of the Babylonian Talmud, once in Abot d'Rabbi Nathan, and once in the Tractate Baba Batra:

> Hillel the Elder had eighty disciples: thirty of them were worthy that the Divine Presence should rest upon them as upon Moses our teacher, but their generation was not worthy of it; thirty of them were worthy that the intercalation of the years should be determined by them; and twenty were average. The greatest of them all was Jonathan ben Uzziel, and the least of them was Johanan ben Zakkai. . . . [cf. Supplement: Johanan ben Zakkai #1 & 2]

So you see, Johanan ben Zakkai was at the bottom of the class! Some bottom of the class! Some class! What we are being told in effect is something like this: "Look, if Johanan was the least of the disciples of Hillel, what a mighty group they all were!"

Johanan can be viewed as a moderate. In fact, though he is part of the coterie that concerned itself with mysticism tinged with the apocalyptic, he did not go along with it with respect to instant messianism. This is never explicitly stated. It comes out very subtly.

The reference to Rabban Johanan in Abot d'Rabbi Nathan tells us something about his training after we are informed about his so-called "mediocrity":

> It was said of Rabbi Johanan ben Zakkai that he mastered Scripture, Mishnah, Gemarah, *halakhot, aggadot, toseftot*, the minutiae of the Torah, the minutiae of the Scribes, and all the hermeneutical rules of the sages. . . .
> [cf. Supplement: Johanan ben Zakkai #1]

Scripture had not yet been canonized as the Bible [that was done under his leadership]; the Mishnah was not written down until a century later [it was in the making]; and the Talmuds, Palestinian and Babylonian, were not codified until the fourth and seventh centuries. But no matter, here the accepted curriculum of the sage is being recorded by later traditions.

However, when you look at the sources in Sukka and Baba Batra, which are almost identical, here is what we see:

> They said of Rabbi Johanan ben Zakkai that he did not leave unstudied Scripture, Mishnah, Gamara, *Halakha, Aggada* details of the Torah, details of the scribes, inferences *a minori ad majus*, analogies, calendrical computations, *gematrias* the speech of Ministering Angels, the speech of spirits, and the speech of palm trees, fuller's fables and fox fables, great matters and small matters. Great matters mean *ma'aseh merkava*, small matters, the discussions of Abaye and Rava. [cf. Supplement: Johanan ben Zakkai #2]

The one listing excludes all subjects touching on mysticism, magic and theurgy, and anything that smacks of gnosticism. The other two include it. Clearly we can see reflected here the disapproval of anything that smacked of instant messianism in the Abot d'Rabbi Nathan passage, and no particular objection in the other two.

When we remember that the debacle of the year 70 was followed by the even more traumatic debacle of the failure of the Bar Kochba revolt in the year 135, we can perhaps theorize that by this time apocalyptic concerns and messianic studies were seen as dangerous and to be avoided.

We find a similar indication in another source about Johanan ben Zakkai. In the Abot d' Rabbi Nathan passage that omits the listing of apocalyptic and mystical curricula in the account of Rabbi Johanan's study curriculum, we have another interesting episode.

A young son of Johanan's, who was a promising young scholar, had died, and Johanan's disciples, five of them, two of whom we shall meet in the next chapter, came to console him. They included his most brilliant student, El'azar ben Arakh, scholar and mystic, of whom it was written that when birds flew over the place where he studied the secrets of creation, birds flying overhead were scorched!

The first four students who tried their hand at consolation used the same approach and were rebuffed. Each tried to console Johanan by telling him that the same thing had happened to some great person preceding him—Adam, Job, Aaron and David. "What has that to do with my pain?" he retorted.

Only El'azar ben Arak, that brilliant young apocalyptic mystic, succeeded. He used the metaphor of a king entrusting a servant with a precious article. When the King came to take it back, what could the subject do? "You have comforted me," says Johanan.

So El'azar ben Arak emerges on top. Good, you say? Now he will emerge as a successor to Johanan? Not at all. Let us see what follows:

> When they left his presence Rabbi El'azar said to his colleagues, "I will go to Dimsith, a delectable spot with excellent and refreshing waters." The others said, "We will go to Yavneh, a place abounding with scholars and lovers of Torah." Because he went to Dimsith, a delectable spot with excellent and refreshing waters, his fame in the Torah waned; whereas they who went to Yavneh,

a place abounding with scholars and lovers of the Torah, their renown in Torah increased. [cf. Supplement:
Johanan ben Zakkai #3]

This is a strange appendage to a story that celebrates El'azar's
excellence and apparent primacy. He scores with Johanan, but
does not go to Yavneh to participate in the great seminal act of
Johanan ben Zakkai. What is happening here?

Dimsith is the crucial word, for it was another name by
which Emmaus was known. Now it becomes clear, for Emmaus
was an important center for early Christians and instant messianists. The statement that El'azar went to Dimsith while the others
went to Yavneh is a subtle, almost unnoticeable manner of expression in which the parting of the ways between early Christianity and Rabbinic Judaism, out of their common roots, was
referred to!

The trauma of the defeat by the Romans, the destruction of
Jerusalem and the Temple, which was deeply sensed and perhaps explains the intensity of the efforts of the Sages to shape a
Judaism that could survive it, is deep and searing. It might well
have had such a paralyzing impact that survival might have been
impossible. How could one go on with the Temple destroyed and
God defeated?

Johanan showed the way. If there were no longer sacrifices,
there could be prayer and loving kindness;

It once happened [we read in Abot d'Rabbi Nathan
IV:1] that Rabban Johanan ben Zakkai was coming out
of Jerusalem, followed by Rabbi Joshua, and he beheld
the Temple in ruins. "Woe is us," cried Rabbi Joshua,
"for this house that lies in ruins, the place where atonement was made for the sins of Israel!" Rabban Johanan
said to him, "My son, be not grieved, for we have another means of atonement which is as effective, and
that is the *practice of loving kindness* . . . and what is the
practice of loving kindness? He provided for the bride . . .
attended the dead to the grave, gave alms to the poor

and *prayed three times a day.* [cf. Supplement: Johanan ben Zakkai #4]

Prayer could replace sacrifice. And Johanan had the sensitivity to show the way.

The move to Yavneh was crucial. There is a difference of opinion among scholars as to whether Johanan chose Yavneh and took the leadership there with him, or whether Yavneh was where they were forced to go because it was a place of internment for those Jews who gave up the fight, while the battle continued in other parts of the country.

Whichever theory is accepted, what is nevertheless certain is that when Johanan and the sages went to Yavneh and did there what they did, that act was crucial and is so remembered in the Talmudic traditions.

We do not know for certain exactly what happened at Yavneh, but we know both from outside sources and from Talmudic traditions that here was the center of the rallying forces for Jewish survival. What came out of Yavneh, what Jewish tradition associates with Yavneh, was of enormous consequence.

It is helpful to list them:

The seat of the Sanhedrin was moved to Yavneh and Gamaliel II was rescued from Jerusalem, continuing the Hillelite leadership in the Patriarchate. His father, Simeon ben Gamliel, had perished in the siege.

The final organization of the liturgy for daily worship and the structure of the Passover Seder, separated from the Temple service, yet redolent with its memories, was fixed.

The process of the canonization of the Bible was completed, and the books of the Apocrypha with their heavy apocalyptic overtones were excluded from the canon, as though to underscore the commitment to long range messianism.

The institution of a prayer against the oppressing government, and the heretics who threatened the authenticity and integrity of the survival pattern developed by the sages, the prayer against the *minim*, was introduced into the core of prayer. This was also directed against Jewish Christians and marked the beginning of the separation of the two groups within Judaism. By this time the earliest versions of the gospels were beginning to circulate.

We have the record of a number of other decisions, or *takanot* as they are called, that illustrate steps taken to cope with realities. For example, with the Temple destroyed, and Priests and Levites among the exiles, how could they survive? Though the Temple service no longer existed, it was decreed that tithes continue to be paid so that they could be fed. And reflective of a desperate effort to protect the declining economy, the herding of "small cattle," that is, sheep and goats was forbidden in order to protect what remained of the lands for cultivation.

Some purely temple ceremonials were perpetuated, even though the Temple lay in ruins in order to preserve the most colorful and inspirational aspects of public celebration. During Sukkot, one of the three pilgrim festivals, the people would come up to Jerusalem for the seven day festival carrying the *lulav,* the combination of palm, myrtle, willow and citron. In Jerusalem and on the Temple grounds it was to be carried for all seven days. In the provinces only one day was required. That was when the Temple stood.

What do we read about Johanan in this instance?

> Beforetime the *lulav* was taken in hand the entire seven days of Tabernacles, but in the provinces one day only. After the Temple was destroyed, Rabban Johanan ben Zakkai ordained that it should be taken the full seven days in the provinces, in memory of the Temple. [cf. Supplement: Johanan ben Zakkai #12]

To this very day, when the Jew carries the lulav for the seven days of Sukkot, he remembers. Johanan was one of the central architects of that remembering.

But after all is said and done, it is the moment of decision by Johanan and how it is recorded especially in the tradition of Talmudic memory that concerns us here, and that we shall now examine. Jerusalem is besieged, and the resistance mounts to its bloody crescendo. Johanan decides to leave the city, to negotiate with the Romans for a breathing spell.

How is this to be viewed? Is he a traitor, deserting the resistance forces? Or has he seen that resistance is doomed to fail, and another course must be taken? Does he negotiate with the Emperor as an equal, or does he come before the Emperor as a prisoner of war? Does he pick Yavneh or does he find himself there against his will? Did the Romans really want to destroy Jerusalem, or did the stubborn, irrational resistance of the zealots force the issue?

The existing historical sources give a variety of views. Josephus, one of the best contemporary sources, closest to the events, tries to exculpate the Romans. He has, after all, by going over to the conquerors, become their public relations representative. And after the bitterness of the end of the war, he tries to improve the image of his masters. In his account of the conference with his generals [which included Tiberias Alexander, Philo's nephew who had gone over to the Romans], Titus is seen as opposed to the destruction of the Temple. In his War of the Jews we read:

> Now some thought it would be best . . . to demolish it. . . . Others were of the opinion that he might save it. . . . But Titus said that he was not . . . for burning down [the Temple] because this would be a mischief to the Romans themselves, as it would be an ornament to their government while it continued. [cf. Reinach, p. 394]

Josephus goes even further in his apologia. He tells us that when over-zealous soldiers set fire to the Temple against his orders, Titus gave the command to have the fires extinguished.

It takes rabbinic memory as recorded in the Talmud, and the memory of a Christian monk who preserves an account of Tacitus otherwise lost, to set the record straight.

The account of Tacitus describing the situation in Jerusalem and the circumstances surrounding the decision to destroy the Temple have already been mentioned. There it is clearly stated that it was Titus who opted for the destruction of the Temple. That particular passage was preserved for posterity from a lost portion of Tacitus' *Historiae* by a fourth century monk, Sulpicius Severus.

The Rabbinic traditions preserved in the Talmud are equally clear. There we read:

> Vespasian sent Titus [against Jerusalem after he left for Rome to assume the Emperor's mantle]. Titus said: "Where is their God, the rock in whom they trusted?" This was the wicked Titus who blasphemed and insulted Heaven. What did he do? He took a harlot by the hand and entered the Holy of Holies and spread out a scroll of the Torah and committed a sin upon it. . . . [Supplement: Johanan ben Zakkai #6]

This is hardly evidence for Titus' defense of the Temple!

There are four different places in Rabbinic literature where the traditions about the destruction of the Temple and Johanan's move to Yavneh are recorded. One version is found in Gittin, two in Abot d'Rabbi Nathan, and one in the *Midrash*, Lamentations Rabbah. They differ in details, as an examination of the various texts describing this event in the Appendix will demonstrate. In one we see Johanan before Vespasian as an equal; in another he is treated with suspicion and thrown into prison. In one he appears in friendly contact with the Romans while still in besieged Jerusalem; in another he does not seem to be at all opposed to the Zealots.

In one he is hostile to the Zealots; in another he is represented as being related to their chief. In one he arranges his escape alone; in another, the leader of the Zealots, apparently sympathetic to him, helps him to escape. There are even variants in what he asks of Vespasian. In one case he asks for Yavneh and its scholars. In another he asks for just enough time to rescue people close to him.

But taken all-in-all, its collective impact shows how deeply the event engraved itself upon the national consciousness. It is expressed, as so much significant historical experience of the people is expressed, in the form of what can be described as agadic archaeology. Such Talmud texts become important historical sources for us, and we shall observe it particularly through the medium of the Gittin passage.

Let us look at it for a moment. It begins with an account of beleaguered Jerusalem in the hands of the Zealots. The sages felt that the time was ripe to go out to the Romans. However, the leader of the Zealots, Abba Sikra summons Johanan:

> "Come visit me privately" [came the message]. When he came [Johanan] said, "How long are you going to carry on this way and kill all the people with starvation?" He replied: "What can I do? If I say a word to them, they will kill me." He said: "Devise a plan for me to escape. Perhaps I shall be able to save a little." [cf. Supplement: Johanan Ben Zakkai #6]

Abba Sikra then arranges the strategem for Johanan's escape and he comes to Vespasian. There follows a dialogue wherein Johanan hails Vespasian as King, and Vespasian taxes him for coming so late. Then comes the news from Rome, during the interview, announcing him Emperor. Then the Emperor says:

> "I am now going and will send someone to take my place. You can however make a request of me and I shall grant it." He said to him: "Give me Yavneh and its Wise Men, and the family chain of Rabban Gamaliel." Rabbi Akiba said: "He ought to have said to him, 'Let the Jews off this time.' " He however thought that so much he would not grant, and so even a little would not be saved. [ibid.]

Then follows the vivid details, in all their horror, of the intrusion of Titus into the Holy of Holies, the desecration and sacking of the Temple and the burning of Jerusalem.

For no matter what the details, no matter what the role of others may have been, in folk memory, in folk tradition Johanan emerges as the central figure, and the move to Yavneh as his central act.

Here it is our purpose to illustrate how Rabbinic texts, despite the variants we encounter, represent a very useful, perhaps central source for mining the details of Jewish historical experience.

For the traditions, orally presented in the schools, and ultimately written down in all their spontaneous variety, are really more than archaeological relics or geological fossils, important though such may be. They are the very stuff of life. The juices of a vital and contemporary experience run through them.

With respect to the variant traditions describing Johanan's escape from Jerusalem, his meeting with Vespasian, and his move to Yavneh with its consequences, we have seen various traditions of the one city and two events—Jerusalem and Yavneh and the Romans in the year 70 CE, and Jerusalem and the Babylonians in the year 586 BCE.

Indeed, we shall see not only varying traditions about the same event, but we shall see the transformation of one tradition into another, and hence see how the patterns of Jewish perceptions of crucial events in Jewish history take this strange and intriguing form of communication.

We find that the very same legend told about Johanan ben Zakkai and Yavneh is told about Jeremiah and Jerusalem. The latter legend pairs Jeremiah with Nebuchadnezzar; the former, of course, pairs Johanan with Vespasian.

Here is how the Jeremiah legend goes:

In their boyhood days, Jeremiah and Nebuchadnezzar were close friends. They would take long walks together and talk about everything under the sun. At this time, Nebuchadnezzar was poor, lowly and despised. One time, he suddenly said to Jeremiah: "I wish I could become king of the world. If I ever did, I would go up against Jerusalem, burn the Temple and the city, kill the inhabitants, and take the rest of the population captive to Babylonia!"

Jeremiah knew [because of his prophetic insight] that this was no idle dream, and that fortune would smile on Nebuchadnezzar and that this would really come about. Jeremiah therefore said to him: "Spare Jerusalem!" "No!" retorted Nebuchadnezzar. "Then spare the Temple!" countered the prophet-to-be. "Can't do it!" replied the king-to-be. "How about the Sanhedrin?" countered Jeremiah. Another no.

In desperation, Jeremiah tries again: "Well, what will you grant me?" "Whatever you can save from the city between midday and dusk," was the final promise. Hence when the city was about to be destroyed, Jeremiah hurried there, but could not get there until after dusk and was unable to rescue a soul. Which, says the tradition, is why he cried out: "Alas for us the day is declining, the shadows of evening grow long." [Jeremiah 6:4]

It takes no wild stretch of the imagination to see the parallel between the Nebuchadnezzar/Jeremiah episode and the Vespasian/Johanan account that we have in four separate versions in the Talmud. The eve of disaster, the prophet or sage predicting that that victor would become Emperor and destroy the city, and finally the plea for the city. Even Josephus tries to get into the act with a similar claim: That he foretold, in the presence of Vespasian, that he, Vespasian, would become Emperor.

Clearly this account was floating around, and when the account of the destruction of Jerusalem was being prepared, it appropriately is used to describe Johanan's role.

This same story, presumably derived from the Nebuchadnezzar/Jeremiah account, crops up in Islam. An eighteenth century Jewish scholar finds this legend in a tenth century Islamic source:

> A certain Jew had a dream in which he saw that the Temple would one day be destroyed by an orphaned child of a widowed mother, whose name was Buchnezzar, so he went to see him. The lad had been in the forest cutting firewood, and he came back to the house with the bundle on his shoulder that he put down. The man talked with him and gave him three drachmae and told him to buy food, and they all dined. This they did for three days. Said the Jew: "Give me a letter of friendship for some day you will be king." "You are making fun of me," said Buchnezzar, "but I will give you a letter." Later he became King, and when he came to Jerusalem to destroy the Temple, the Jew presented the letter, and he was allowed to save his kin. [cf. H.I.D. Azulai, Midbar Kadmut, Jeremiah]

We see the fascinating interweaving of legend and fact around one of the most central, traumatic experiences of the Jewish people, experiences of holocaust proportions. And we see how they are applied in the telling of that history.

In the case of Johanan ben Zakkai, we have four versions that are preserved. In the version in Lamentations Rabba, Johanan is recorded as asking exactly what Jeremiah asked for—the minimal. However, in the Gittin passage, he asks for Yavneh and its scholars. Some later sages felt that he had not asked enough, that he should have requested the sparing of Jerusalem. Scholars even suggest that Johanan did not really ask for the scholars.

But the fact that the request for Yavneh and its scholars is included reflects the emphasis that the sages who recorded this felt about the role of the sages in the survival process. This is after all what Johanan was about, what he intended, and what he achieved.

They said concerning Rabban Johanan ben Zakkai that

> during his whole life he never uttered profane talk, nor walked four cubits without studying the Torah or without *tefillin*, nor was any man earlier than he in the academy, nor did he sleep or doze in the academy, nor did he meditate in filthy alleyways, nor did he leave any one in the academy when he went out, nor did anyone ever find him sitting doing nothing, but only sitting and learning. [cf. Supplement: Johanan ben Zakkai #13]

To summarize: Another step has been taken in the development of the process of Rabbinic Judaism, and thus far we have spanned the crisis of the near-extinction of the Pharisaic/Rabbinic sages, which Simeon ben Shetah turned around, which Hillel continued, and which Johanan ben Zakkai, with that Pharisaic/Rabbinic group in the full measure of its creative powers, carries beyond another extinction threat.

We have looked at the moment of destruction through the eyes of a contemporary Jewish historian, Josephus, a contemporary Roman historian, Tacitus, and Rabbinic sources. We looked at the struggle between extremes and moderates in the Jewish fold. We examined the early evidences of tensions between instant and long range messianism. We saw Johanan teach that prayer could take the place of sacrifice. We saw him rescue a descendant of Hillel to continue the chain of leadership. We saw the crucial acts of Yavneh, the canonization of the scriptures, the organization of the prayer book, and the series of important takanot, or decisions, that set Judaism on its path to survival. And, finally, we saw a glimpse of how agada wrapped its aura around the experience and recorded historical experience of the Jewish people, as it moved forward to fulfill its future.

We will see how the two disciples, Eliezer and Joshua, who carried Johanan from Jerusalem in a coffin to his historic interview with Vespasian and the critical move to Yavneh, carried the process further.

Through an examination of these two personalities we will gain an insight to the social differences of the time—the struggle for and the achievement of democracy within the Sanhedrin, and some glimpses into the relations between early Rabbinic Judaism and early Christianity as we come to the end of the first post-Christian century.

Chapter Six

Eliezer and Joshua

We turn our attention now to the two disciples at either end of the coffin who carried Johanan ben Zakkai out of Jerusalem to his rendezvous with Vespasian.

It was that rendezvous that changed the course of Jewish history. It was that rendezvous that led to Yavneh, and from Yavneh to the powerful flow forward of Rabbinic Judaism.

Ben Zakkai's most promising and brilliant student, El'azar ben Arak, went to Emmaus and not to Yavneh, and was lost to the movement. Eliezer and Joshua were close to their master, remained with him, and carried on in his spirit.

They were in every sense an "odd couple." The one was a follower of Shammai, the other of Hillel. The one was the son of a millionaire landowner, and was himself wealthy. The other was a man of the people, out of the lower middle classes. The one had a fine presence and an imposing bearing. The other is remembered for his ugliness. The one was conservative, the other democratic in spirit. But they had one thing in common—a commitment to the process and a brilliant capacity to shape it.

A word must be said about the symbolism of opposites at either end of a coffin that carried within it the living hopes for survival. Two opposites and a coffin equal survival? This is a proposition that is difficult to believe. Nevertheless the Jewish answer is clearly yes. It is an answer that comes out of the deep Pharisaic belief in resurrection as a cardinal tenet of the Jewish faith that envisioned the conquest over death and destruction.

For the long range messianism that became Rabbinic Judaism, it bespoke the phoenix-like rise from the death of the corporate Jewish people in its march through history. For the short range messianism that became Christianity, it bespoke the conviction that the transformation from death to hope through the experience of the central figure in its saga was the redemptive way to the future.

So the image of the coffin and the image of the cross play a crucial symbolic role in the gestation of the siblings.

Let us return to the men on either side of the coffin. Eliezer and Joshua, opposites in so many ways, embodied the dialectic within developing Rabbinic Judaism, inherent in the process of Rabbinic Judaism. This process, already underway, went to Yavneh in defeat. In Yavneh, the varying strains and tendencies yet unresolved were brought together under the umbrella of the dialectic process where differences could live together. What emerged was the transition from a Temple and priest-oriented Judaism to a Rabbinic Sage and synagogue-oriented Judaism.

It should be noted that the terms Pharisee-Scribe-Sage-Rabbi are used interchangeably, because our focus is constantly on the process, and the one is always the other in the process. There are scholars who tend to see the Pharisees as the group under oral law linked more closely to the Temple, while Johanan ben Zakkai concentrates on leading the change to synagogue/rabbi/sage. Scholars also see Johanan as leading the process that made it possible for other sects, like the Sadducees, to find their place with developing Judaism.

Despite all this, it is the process that is the focus for us, and we must keep our eye on this broader picture. Hence the spotlight now rests on Joshua and Eliezer. The struggle in which they were involved made for a crucial turn in the development of Rabbinic Judaism. It was a turn in the direction of democratization, of majority rule in the Sanhedrin. It was a turn away from those who looked to autocratic leadership reminiscent of Temple times, reflecting Sadducaic and Shammaite viewpoints. Through Joshua the Hillelites gained ascendancy. It was also, perhaps, a victory of the middle classes over the upper classes; of the thrust to change over the instinct to look back and hold back; and, finally, of the long-range messianic impulse within Rabbinic Judaism over the short-range messianic thrust.

The episode of the Oven of Aknai and the defeat of Eliezer,

which has already been referred to as one of the examples of theological decision through *midrash*, is crucial here and we must begin by returning to it briefly.

Eliezer has become presiding officer of the Sanhedrin, its Nasi. He is recognized as the outstanding repository of halakhah. Long before the computer age, he retained all the traditions that had preceded him in his photographic memory. He could bring them up at will. His teacher, Johanan ben Zakkai, had recognized this and described him as "a cemented cistern that loses not a drop" and "a glazed pitcher that preserves its wine."

Hence, when in the case of the ruling on the ritual purity of the oven his views were opposed persistently, "all that day" we are told, he found it necessary, in desperation, to turn to a series of miracles to assert his authority. He invokes miracle after miracle, and the opposition led by Joshua keeps saying "No!"

Does he make a tree jump, water flow uphill, walls totter? No matter. Does he invoke a voice from heaven, a bat kol? Not in heaven, is the response. Shall we recall the text for a moment?

> On that day Rabbi Eliezer brought forward every imaginable argument, but they did not accept them. "If the halakhah agrees with me let this carob tree prove it!" Thereupon the carob tree was torn a hundred cubits out of its place. "No proof can be brought from a carob tree" they rejoined. Again he said to them: "If the halakhah agrees with me let this stream of water prove it!" whereupon the stream of water flowed backwards. "No proof can be adduced from a stream of water," they rejoined. . . . [cf. Supplement: Eliezer ben Hyrcanus #5]

As a Chicagoan I cannot resist an aside about the river flowing backward. That is what was done in Chicago to prevent sewage from flowing into Lake Michigan, and so the Chicago River flows upstream into the sewage canal! Shades of Eliezer's miracle. One thing they have in common in the matter of clean and unclean! But back to the oven of Aknai and to the rejected miracles in the process of the struggle for democracy.

That amazing gesture of Joshua, pointing heavenward and proclaiming: *"Lo bashamayim hi* [it is not in heaven]," followed by God's good-humored acceptance of His defeat by mortals, makes the point. Eliezer, who stands for autocratic authority over democratic consensus, is defeated. He is not only defeated, but excommunicated as well. He loses his power. The power has shifted, and the direction is new.

There is something else involved in the "not in heaven" cry. Not only is the victory of the Hillelites over the Shammaites achieved, and not only the final rejection of the Sadducaic/ Temple view, but it is also a repudiation of Eliezer's close and friendly attitude to early Christianity, and a rejection of the early Christian claims at the time when the first gospels were already circulating.

When Joshua cries out "It is not in heaven," what did he mean, asked the text. Said Rabbi Jeremiah: "[He meant] that the Torah had already been given on Mount Sinai and we pay no attention to a heavenly voice because Thou hast long since written in the Torah at Mount Sinai 'After the majority must one incline' " [B. Baba Batra 59a].

Early Christianity was proclaiming itself as a new revelation and was justifying itself through miracles. Here, from the immediate post-Yavneh period, is another indication from the rabbinic side of direct contact between the two siblings at the early period of their development. But more of that later.

Let us now look more closely at the disciples on either side of that historic coffin. Eliezer was of aristocratic background. His father Hyrcanus was one of the four richest men of the time. The other three are named in the account: Ben Zizit Hakkeshet, Nakdimon ben Gorion, and Ben Kalba Sabua. The latter, who is the father-in-law of Rabbi Akiba, whom we shall meet in the next chapter, is described in connection with the siege of Jerusalem as resisting the efforts of the Zealot leaders to carry out a scorched earth policy against the Romans.

You may recall that Hillel came to the study of Torah as a poor man. For Eliezer, the situation was reversed. He gave up a life of luxury and well-being to devote himself to the scholarly life. His was a case of riches to rags. When he announced to his father Hyrcanus that he wished to leave the estates and study Torah with Johanan ben Zakkai, Hyrcanus took a very dim view of the matter. In fact he threatened to disinherit him.

> What was the beginning of Rabbi Eliezer ben Hyrcanus? He was twenty-two years old and had not yet studied Torah [we read in the Abot d'Rabbi Nathan 20b]. One day he said to his father: "I will go and study Torah under Rabban Johanan ben Zakkai." His father Hyrcanus replied: "You shall not taste a morsel of food until you have ploughed a complete furrow." [cf. Supplement: Eliezer ben Hyrcanus #1]

Like an obedient son, Eliezer plowed the furrow, but he did not come home for dinner. Instead, hungry and unfed, he made his way to the academy of Johanan ben Zakkai. He studied on an empty stomach, and because he had not eaten, those around him became aware of his offensive breath. In fact, Johanan asked him whether he had eaten and received an evasive reply. The truth came out and he was finally fed, and then Johanan said to him:

> "Just as an offensive smell came forth from your mouth, so shall there go forth from you a distinguished name in Torah." [ibid.]

Hillel is dug up out of a mound of snow on the roof on the Sabbath; Eliezer emerges from an evil smelling fog of hunger to brilliance in learning. Rabbinic tradition took great delight in showing how the sages struggled to achieve learning.

Eliezer had been disinherited, yet he went on to become one of the outstanding disciples of his outstanding master. His brilliant memory, and the encyclopedic character of the Halakhah which he remembers, rapidly led him to center stage.

In the meantime, Hyrcanus was determined to disinherit

Eliezer publicly, and set out to confront him in the academy. Johanan gave orders that he not be admitted. We are informed:

> When he came in and wished to sit down, they did not allow him to do so, and he was compelled to move forward until he came to where Ben Zizit Hakkeshet, Nakdimon ben Gorion, and Ben Kalba Sabua were seated, and he sat down among them trembling. It was said that on that day Rabban Johanan ben Zakkai turned his gaze upon Rabbi Eliezer and bade him to commence the discourse. . . . [ibid.]

Eliezer, seeing his father enter, was terrified. He declined to speak, but was urged on by his fellow students and persuaded to begin. He performed brilliantly. His teacher embraced him, praised him highly, and then:

> Hyrcanus stood up and said: "My masters, I came here for the sole purpose of depriving my son Eliezer by vow of my property, but now I declare all my property assigned to my son Eliezer." [ibid.]

The evidences of Eliezer's patrician and conservative background are varied, and several texts bring them out in interesting fashion. In Mishnah [7:7] to the Tractate Pe'ah which deals with the rights of the poor to the unharvested corner of the fields and of the gleanings, we read:

> If a vineyard consists entirely of defective clusters, Rabbi Eliezer says it belongs to the owner, but Rabbi Akiba [whose wife left the household of her wealthy father Ben Kalba Sabua to share Akiba's poverty] says it belongs to the poor. [cf. Supplement: Eliezer ben Hyrcanus #3]

The passing references to his wealth are clear. We learn that he owned slaves from a reference to the death of his slave Tabi, and from his refusal to accept the consolation of his disciples, because a slave was to be considered property and not a person under the law. In the account from Berakhot 16b, we see how he avoids his disciples who come to console him, and how they persist:

> Our Rabbis taught: For male and female slaves no row of comforters is formed, nor is the blessing of mourners said, nor is condolence offered. When the bondwoman of Rabbi Eliezer died, his disciples went in to condole with him. When he saw them he went up to an upper chamber but they went up with him. He went to an anteroom and they followed him there. He went to the dining room and they followed him there. . . . [cf. Supplement: Eliezer ben Hyrcanus #2]

Finally, he faces them, and rebukes them with the words: "I thought you would be scalded with warm water. I see that you are not scalded even with boiling water." And then he gave them the halakhic answer. It is clear to me that the persistence of the disciples in wishing to offer condolence came from their perception of the bondwoman as a human being whose death was worthy of being mourned. So much for the patrician side of Eliezer.

Joshua came from the other side of the social scale. He came from the humble folk, spoke for them and to them. He would very naturally oppose the dictatorial authority of the upper classes, and it is no accident that he was the leader of the opposition in the events around the Oven of Aknai, when he proclaimed his resounding: "Lo bashamayim hi!" [It is not in heaven!]

In the Talmud Tractate Ta'anit there is a discussion on how the Torah may be likened to water or wine. On observing the principle of gravity, where water flows from a higher level to a lower level, the sages conclude: "The words of Torah endure only with him who is meek-minded." In this context, Rabbi Joshua is introduced with the following episode:

> This is illustrated by the story of the daughter of the Emperor who addressed Rabbi Joshua ben Hananiah:

"O glorious wisdom in an ugly vessel!" He replied: "Does not your father keep wine in an earthenware vessel?" She asked: "Wherein else shall he keep it?" He replied: "You who are noble should keep it in vessels of gold and silver." [cf. Supplement: Joshua ben Hananiah #2]

The Princess asks the Emperor to do this and the wine goes sour. Angrily the Emperor challenges him:

"Why did you give her such advice?" He replied: "I answered her the way she spoke to me." "But are there not good looking people who are learned?" "If these people were ugly they would be more learned!" [ibid.]

This then is Rabbi Joshua's attitude to the "beautiful people." The struggle in relation to Torah and social status runs through the whole course of Jewish history. Medieval preachers coming from the lower social levels made much of the Talmudic comment that a "mamzer" [bastard] who was a scholar outranked a High Priest who was an ignoramus! And then of course we have the conflict between the Hasidim and the Mitnagdim in eighteenth century Poland, pitting the unlettered and disenfranchised against the intellectual educated class of the privileged.

This attitude of Rabbi Joshua's is underscored by his remark that no one had ever gotten the better of him except a woman, a little boy and a little girl. In the first case he was rebuked because he forgot to leave her a tip after she had served him lunch. In the other it had to do with his not listening to their directions properly. In any case it represents an attitude far removed from the patrician way of looking on the world. [cf. Babylonian Talmud, Erubin 54a]

This is also reflected in his capacity to communicate with the common folk effectively, because he understood them so well. Unlike Eliezer, whom we just saw retreating from his students until he was finally cornered and compelled to give them an answer, Joshua was accessible and immensely empathetic.

Shortly after the destruction of Jerusalem and the Temple,

and in the early years of the Yavneh period, there was a moment when it seemed that the Emperor would relent and permit the rebuilding of the Temple. A flurry of excitement and anticipation went through the Jewish world and great throngs prepared to return. But there was intervention by forces hostile to the Jewish people and the order was rescinded. Anticipation turned to anger, and anger to preparation for a new war.

To prevent such a suicidal development the Sages dispatched Joshua to the scene. That he was chosen for the mission speaks volumes for the kind of person he was. We read the account as preserved in the Midrash Genesis Rabbah [LXIV:10]:

> Thereupon the Sages decided: "Let a wise man go and pacify the congregation. Then let Rabbi Joshua b. Hananiah go as he is a master of scripture." [cf. Supplement: Joshua ben Hananiah #2]

They select a good darshan [popular preacher] for the task.

So Joshua goes, and with his eloquence, wit and empathy defuses the crisis. He does it with a parable—a technique endemic to the preaching process as developed by Rabbinic Judaism and which Jesus of Nazareth came to use with striking effect:

> So he went and harangued them: A wild lion killed an animal and a bone stuck in his throat. Thereupon he proclaimed: "I will reward anyone who removes it." An Egyptian heron, which has a long beak, came and pulled it out, and demanded his reward. "Go", he replied, "you will be able to boast that you entered the lion's mouth in peace and came out in peace." Even so let us be satisfied that we entered into dealings with this people in peace, and emerged in peace. [ibid.]

Here then is a view of the men at either end of the coffin, of the men at either end of the social scale, of the men at either end of the dialectic. Though antagonists and opposites to each other, they were as one in shaping the process and continuing the march to survival.

In these immediate post-Yavnian years, as Rabbinic Judaism, with its basically long range messianic outlook is taking shape, early Christianity is also taking form. The earliest gospels are circulating. The two sects within Judaism widen the gap between them and begin to move apart. So far as the Romans are concerned, however, they are dealing with Jews and Judaism, and they see no difference between the two. As Tacitus reports Titus to have said, to destroy Judaism the root would be to destroy Judaism the branch. It is through Eliezer and Joshua that we see evidence of this contact in the process of separation.

While Eliezer was still *Nasi* of the post-Yavneh Council of Sages, he was arrested by the Roman authorities and accused of *Minuth*, which is to say, participation in the Christian Sect. This was seen by the Romans as equally revolutionary, as were the recently defeated Zealots. Upon being questioned, he fenced with the Roman Governor, who asked him: "How can a Sage like you occupy yourself with such things?"

To this Eliezer replied: "I acknowledge the Judge as right." The Governor thought he was referring to the secular power when in fact he was referring to God. Upon being released, he went home, but was inconsolable that he was taken for a Christian. The account in Abodah Zarah [16b] continues:

> His disciples called upon him to console him, but he would accept no consolation. Said Rabbi Akiba to him: "Master, wilt thou permit me to say one thing of what thou hast taught me?" He replied: "Say it." "Master, perhaps some of the teaching of the *Minim* had been transmitted to thee and thou didst approve of it, and because of that thou wast arrested?" He exclaimed: "Akiba, thou hast reminded me. I was once walking in the upper market of Sepphoris when [I came across one of the disciples of Jesus the Nazarene] Jacob of K'far Sekania by name who said to me: It is written in your Torah: *You shall not bring the fee of a whore or the pay of a dog into the house of the Lord your God.* [Deut. 23:19] May such money be applied to the erection of a privy for the High Priest? To which I made no reply. Said he to me: *For they were amassed from*

fees for harlotry and they shall become harlot's fees again. [Micah 1:7] These words pleased me very much and that is why I was arrested for apostasy. For in that way I transgressed the scriptural admonition *Remove your way far from her*—which refers to *minuth*—*and do not come near to the doors of her house* [Prov. 5:8]—which refers to the ruling power. [cf. Supplement: Eliezer ben Hyrcanus #4]

Here we see the account of an encounter of a Tannaitic sage of the Yavneh period in direct contact with James the Little, one of the disciples of Jesus, and the actual quotation of an alleged teaching by Jesus on the question of ritual purity which was a constant and central issue in the circles of developing Rabbinic Judaism. It also seems to reflect a period of constant interaction and of dialogue.

In the Talmud there are frequent references to debates between Sages and *Minim*, or Sectarians, and frequently it is not easy to determine whether they were gnostics, or pagans, or Zoroasterians. We can, however, determine who the *Min* is by the nature of the debate. If it raises the question about two Gods, it is likely a pagan or a gnostic. If, however, the theme is God's rejection and the passage of the elect status to others, it is usually an early Christian speaking.

Generally speaking, however, in most instances, references to *Minim* would suggest Christians. After the Emperor Constantine became a Christian, direct references in the Talmud to Jesus tended to be avoided. And when they occurred, they were excluded either by Christian censorship which considered them hostile; or Jewish self-censorship in the middle ages, because their inclusion might cause them trouble with the Christian authorities. But they are preserved in older manuscripts, and we have a list of them in a volume called *Hashmatat Hashass* [Excised Passages from the Talmud].

In some instances, however, these references are so garbled that they suggest corrupted traditions in Babylonia, far from direct contact with Christian communities. An example of this is the reference to an encounter with Jesus [Babylonian Talmud, Sotah 47a] by Joshua ben Perahia, a colleague of Simeon ben

Shetah's, who fled to Alexandria, at the time of the persecution of the Pharisees by the King, Alexander Jannai. Since Judah lived in 100 BCE, it is clear that this fourth century Babylonian tradition had a touch of confusion in it.

We have already noted that Joshua was seen as an effective public spokesman for Judaism in the case of the aborted Roman decree on the rebuilding of the Temple. We find him frequently involved in polemics with early Christians. For example [Hagigah 5b]:

> Rabbi Joshua ben Hananiah was once at the court of Caesar. A certain *Min* showed him by gestures: A people whose Lord has turned His face from them. He showed him in reply: His hand is stretched over us. Said Caesar to Rabbi Joshua: "What did he show thee?"—"A people whose Lord has turned his face from them. And I showed him: His hand is stretched over us." [cf. Supplement: Joshua ben Hananiah #4]

The question at issue is very clear. Christians were saying that they were the true Israel, the successors of the mantle of election which the Jewish people had forfeited by their rejection of Jesus. In this account Joshua is described as emerging victorious. For when the *Min* was asked what he had signaled, he gave the answer. But when asked what Joshua replied with his sign, he could not answer. And they said to him: "A man who does not understand what he is being shown by gesture should not hold converse in signs before the King!"

What tradition thought of Joshua on this matter is made clear by how the tradition concludes:

> When the time of Rabbi Joshua's death approached, the Sages said to him: "What will become of us at the hands of the unbelievers?" [ibid.]

They were losing their best spokesperson.

Just to understand the basic cause of these feelings we have only to see what happened when Rabbi Abbahu commended

Rabbi Safra to the *Minim* as a learned man, and as interpreter of Jewish scriptures. They asked him a question about the passage from Amos: "You only have I known from all the families of the earth; therefore I will visit on you all your iniquities." Here early Christians were raising the question of the rejection of the Jew for his sins, and hence a justification of the Christian succession. The account in Aboda Zara [4a] continues:

> He was silent and could give them no answer, so they wound a scarf around his neck and tortured him. Rabbi Abbahu came and found him [in that state] and said to them: "Why do you torture him?" Said they: "Have you not told us that he is a great man? He cannot explain to us the meaning of this verse!" Said he: "I may have told you that he was learned in Halakhah; did I tell you he was learned in Scripture?"

You see, this was a rare talent, and it was a talent that Joshua possessed to an ample degree.

As has already been suggested, this was the period that Rabbinic Judaism and early Christianity were taking shape. By this time, Christianity was beginning to make rapid progress. One of its central theses was Christianity as the successor in God's favor to Judaism. The Esau/Jacob syndrome was reversed, with the Christians assigned the favored role of Jacob, and the Jew becoming Esau! In their view the mantle of Abrahamitic promise and Sinai Covenant had passed to them.

So it was that Tertullian, in his *Adversus Judaeos* could quote a debate between an early Christian and a Jew in which the former interpreted the words of Isaac's blessing that "the younger would rule over the older" as follows:

> Prior et major populus, id est Judaicus, serviat necesse et minori, et minor populus, id est Chriastianus, superet majorem. [The elder is the Jew, the younger is the Christian, and the younger would rule over the elder.] [Tertullian, *Adversus Judaeos* 1]

It was claims such as this that were the probable basis for the idea that in the era preceding the coming of the Messiah insolence and brazenness would increase. The Jerusalem Talmud, closer to these events than the Babylonian, testifies to this:

> Rabbi Aha said in the name of Rabbi Huna: In the world to come the impious Esau will don a *tallit* and will attempt to take his place with the righteous in the Garden of Eden, but God will take hold of him and throw him out. . . . [J. Nedarim III:10]*

So when Eliezer was embroiled in a misunderstanding, and Joshua traded gestures with an Early Christian in the presence of the Emperor, we see clearly the double edged struggle that was in process, between long range and instant messianists within Judaism, and between both, each in their way against the Romans. The siblings were moving apart as they struggled over the mess of their ancestral pottage!

This is expressed very poignantly in the interpretation of a scriptural verse by a colleague of Eliezer and Joshua. El'azar ben Azaria, whom they select to be Nasi when Eliezer ben Hyrcanus is excommunicated, could look at the verse from Deuteronomy [26:17–18]: *You have affirmed this day that the Lord is your God. . . . and the Lord has affirmed this day that you are . . . his treasured people,* and interpret it with this poignant comment:

> You have made me a unique object of your love in the world, and I shall make you a unique object of my love in the world. [Hagigah 3a]

We have come far in the development of Rabbinic Judaism through Simeon ben Shetah, Hillel, Johanan ben Zakkai, Eliezer and Joshua, and now we meet the man who began to consolidate the process, Akiba ben Joseph.

Chapter Seven

Akiba

Akiba can be considered one of the main links in the chain of the development of Rabbinic Judaism.

The evidence for this is not hard to come by. We can point to many sources that assert this. Two examples will suffice.

We have already encountered that well-known episode in the life of Akiba. Moses resists death because he feels it unjust that he was not to be permitted to enter the Promised Land. God finally persuades him to submit to the inevitable if he can be reassured that the Jewish people are in good hands with their future leadership. So he shows him Akiba, and even though he does not understand what he is teaching, it is in his name, and it is valid.

In this tradition Akiba is seen as his successor, in fact as the most important Jew since Moses. Seven or eight hundred years previously, in an attempt to name the most important Jewish leaders up to his time, the prophet Jeremiah could quote God as saying: "If Moses and Samuel would arise and testify for you, I would not listen." [Jer. 15:1] Akiba, it would appear, had succeeded in replacing Samuel in this role.

Clearly this is a tribute to the development of the Oral Law, of Rabbinic Judaism, in the process of development we have been following.

This point about Akiba is made much more directly and in an even more important source, the Midrash Sifrei. Sifrei is one of the earliest of the Midrashim. It dates from the Tannaitic period, probably from the time of Akiba. And if not in Akiba's lifetime, it can certainly be dated not much later than a generation after his death. And there, in a comment on a passage in Deuteronomy 28, we read:

> Had not Shaphan in his time, Ezra in his time and Akiba in his came upon the scene, the Torah would have been forgotten.

Akiba is another one of our "but-for-whoms." He is in a class with Shaphan, who discovers the book of Deuteronomy in the days of Jeremiah, and with Ezra who institutes the regular reading of the Torah and its interpretation after the destruction of the First Temple.

For it is he who takes the next quantum step forward in the development of the Oral Law and its incorporation as a central feature in the development of Rabbinic Judaism.

Let us pick up the trail. Jeremiah sets the process on its course with his letter to the exiles in Babylonia; Ezra, whom we can choose to remember as Malachi/Ezra, is the bridge between the two Commonwealths. By opening the Torah with the process of exegesis to the people, he moves the process forward.

We began our study with Simeon ben Shetah, who saved the process, already two or three centuries in development, from extinction. Hillel shaped the structuring of the exegetic method. Johanan ben Zakkai was the bridge between the end of the Second Commonwealth and Yavneh, into the diaspora. Eliezer and Joshua fought out the battle over the issue of authoritarianism versus democracy.

Now Akiba comes upon the scene to take the decisive step that results in the Mishnah which was the great summing up of Oral Torah in the later stages of the Second Commonwealth. It was a culmination of this period just as the Hebrew Bible represented the same process for the First Commonwealth.

What was it that Akiba did? Not everybody had the encyclopedic memory of an Eliezer ben Hyrcanus. Not everybody could be a lime-lined pit that lost not a drop. There needed to be a better way of remembering the vast body of material in the Oral Law. Akiba found that better way. He developed a method of classification of the material according to major themes and sub-themes.

We have it on the authority of Judah the Prince, the sage who finally edited the Mishnah and who set it in its final form. Speaking of the qualities of his teachers, he described Rabbi Tarphon as a heap of stones, about which it could be said that when you removed one, the rest would come toppling down. So Tarphon, when asked one question in a matter of Torah, would erupt with one gem after another, pell-mell and in no special order.

He described El'azar ben Azariah as a perfumer's chest. He would respond to the disciple with such a wealth of choice knowledge that the disciple would depart feeling laden with every possible variety of fragrant and precious oils.

But he describes Akiba as

> a treasury with compartments. To what may Rabbi Akiba be compared? To a peddler who takes his sack and goes into a field. When he finds wheat he drops it in the sack; similarly when he finds barley, beans and lentils he drops them all in the sack. On returning home he sorts them all out, putting the wheat apart, the barley apart, the beans, the lentils all apart. Such was the practice of Rabbi Akiba. *He sorted all the Torah [he amassed] into its various compartments.* [cf. Supplement: Akiba #17]

No small achievement to have set the structure that shaped the Mishnah. Akiba used his mind like a computer, sorting and organizing. It is he who developed the sixfold division into Zeraim [Seeds], Moed [Festivals], Nashim [Women], Nezikin [Torts and Court Structure], Kodashim [Sanctified Thing] and Toharot [Ritual Cleanness], and their subdivisions into Tractates. It was an enormous achievement.

For the Mishnah as the second pillar for Jewish survival took its place beside the first pillar, Scripture. These two pillars, together with a third, the Siddur [Prayer Book], gave the whole structure a firm base for development. It can be suggested that the long-range messianic wing of their Jewish process emerging at the end of the Second Commonwealth summed itself up with the Mishnah, while the younger Christian sibling did the same with the New Testament. Both based themselves squarely on the Scriptural texts, Torah, Prophets and Writings, that preceded them.

Akiba is responsible for another crucial development. He extended the possibilities of exegesis to its outermost limits. The followers of Shammai depended upon context for their exegesis. Hillel extended it by leaving behind context and placing the emphasis on individual words. Akiba went a step further. You could derive your exegesis not only from a word, but, indeed, from a single letter of the word.

In the account wherein God reassures Moses that the Jewish future would be in good hands with Akiba, we are told:

> He found the Holy One Praised Be He engaged in affixing coronets to the letters [of the Torah]. He said to Him: "Who stays Thy hand?" [i.e. is there anything lacking in the Torah that it needs these additions?] He answered: "There will arise a man at the end of many generations, Akiba ben Joseph by name, who will expound upon each tittle heaps and heaps of Laws!" [cf. Supplement: Akiba #1]

It is Akiba's capacity to exegete even letters and particles of letters that expanded the parameters of interpretation. As a matter of fact, Akiba occupies a special role in Jewish mystical tradition. To him is attributed one of the very important Kabbalistic books entitled *Otiot d'Rabbi Akiba* [The Letters of Rabbi Akiba]. This has to do with the permutation and combination of letters of the alphabet for use in the various secret names of God.

Akiba's extension of the parameters of exegesis was intended to underscore the fact that Torah had to be flexible in order to survive and grow, and flexibility required the extension of the interpretive methods. So, to his emphasis on individual letters, he added an emphasis on seemingly superfluous text elements like "et" [meaning and or with] and "v" [meaning and].

In a real sense he became a proponent of *eisegesis,* reading new meanings into the text.

Akiba's *halakhot* took the realities of life into consideration. In the case of food laws, he always came down on the lenient side, if it made life easier for the people. When Johanan ben Nuri once made a strict decision which would have proved very costly to the ordinary folk, Akiba reproached him, saying: "How long will you waste the money of Israel?" [Ker. 40a]

For Akiba, the dignity of humankind was of paramount importance. For him it even superseded religious custom. "Rather make your Sabbath like a week-day than accept charity" was his dictum.

Akiba not only lives for the Torah. He dies for the Torah. In this sense he goes Moses one step further. The personal tragedy of Moses is that he does not get to enter the Promised Land though he had come down from Mount Sinai with the Torah. Akiba advances Torah to new heights, as the Promised Land comes down in ruins about the people, assures their survival, but dies a martyr's death on their behalf.

Akiba can be seen here as one of the principal martyrs in the history of the Jewish people after the destruction of the Second Commonwealth. The first martyrs to be named are found in the Second Book of Maccabees, as it describes the death of Hannah and her seven sons at the beginning of the Maccabean Revolt. The period begins with martyrdom and it ends with martyrdom.

When in any synagogue, anywhere in the world, a Jew uttering the Shema, the proclamation of God's oneness, takes hold of the fringes of his *Tallit,* places them over his eyes, and prolongs its last word, "ehad!" [one!], he is reenacting what tradition tells us that Akiba did. But more of this a little later.

We have quickly sketched Akiba's achievements: he developed the mold from which the Mishnah was cast; he extended the parameters of exegesis; he contributed to the development of Jewish mysticism, and his martyr-death, his giving up his life to sanctify his faith, becomes the paradigm for future Jewish historical experience.

Unlike Eliezer ben Hyrcanus, but much like Hillel, Akiba was a man of humble origins—probably even more humble than

Hillel. And what is more, he was a late starter. He did not begin his career as a scholar until he had reached the age of forty, and he began as a total ignoramus.

He was a simple unlettered shepherd in the employ of that Jerusalem millionaire, Kalba Sabua, of whom it was said that he was so rich that "whoever entered his house hungry like a dog came out fed to the full." [AbDRN 20b] Rachel, the daughter of his wealthy employer, fell in love with him. When they eloped and were married, she was at once disinherited by her disapproving father.

It was she who inspired Akiba to study, another in that link of extraordinary women who shape great men. When they were courting she said to him: "If we marry will you go away and study?" He assented.

Akiba went off to his studies for twelve years and left his wife behind. She struggled to help support him, and even sold her hair to fund his education. Her neighbors upbraided her for what they considered to be sheer stupidity. Thus when Akiba returned after twelve years with, according to tradition, twelve thousand disciples, he overheard an old man saying to her:

"How long will you lead the life of living widowhood?" "If he would listen to me," she replied, "he would spend another twelve years in study." Said Rabbi Akiba: "It is then with her consent that I am acting," and he departed again and spent another twelve years in the academy. [cf. Supplement: Akiba #3]

Twelve years later he returned in triumph with twenty-four thousand disciples! Rachel's neighbors urged her to borrow fine clothes to greet her husband. "He will recognize me as I am," she said confidently. But as she approached, Akiba's aides thrust her aside. But Akiba intervened:

"Leave her alone! Mine and yours are hers." Her father, hearing that a great man had come to town, said "I shall go to him, and perhaps he will invalidate my vow." When he came to him Rabbi Akiba asked, "Would you have made your vow if you had known he was a great man?" "Had he known," [the father replied] "even one chapter of one single halakhah, [I would not have made the vow]." He then said to him: "I am that man." The other fell on his face, kissed his feet and also gave him half his wealth. [ibid.]

A happy ending indeed to a story that has echoes of the careers of previous sages as reported in Rabbinic tradition. Beginning at age forty, he began teaching in public by the time he was fifty-three, and was so successful, we are told, that

he enjoyed the luxury of tables of silver and gold and ascended his bed by golden steps. His wife went out dressed in fine robes and wearing a golden tiara. [cf. Supplement: Akiba #2]

Seeing this, his astonished disciples cried out: "Master, you put us to shame by the lavish way you treat her!" Clearly they were hearing from their wives. Akiba's retort was simple and direct: "Much hardship has she endured with me for the sake of Torah."

Wife supports husband, husband becomes successful scholar. Akiba's career in this sense mirrors the countless generations of women who sacrificed for the sake of their husbands' careers, and the picture of Rachel walking about with a golden tiara adorning the hair she had once sold to make possible her husband's studies is indeed the crown of glory upon such a relationship and such an achievement.

Akiba becomes such an important role model that he is one of three in a midrash designed to say that neither poverty, nor excess wealth, nor ignorance is an excuse for not studying Torah. For when a person dies and stands before the bar of heavenly judgment, and he has not studied Torah, he will be asked a loud clear "Why?"

If he says, "I was too poor and could not study," they would say, "Were you as poor as Hillel?" and would be reminded of Hillel's achievements, as you should well remember. And if the excuse was: "I was too wealthy and pleasure seeking, and had not time for it," the stern reply would be: "Were you as wealthy and pleasure seeking as Eliezer ben Harsom, yet see what he achieved in Torah." And should the excuse be: "I was too ignorant," the Heavenly Court would thunder: "Were you as ignorant as Akiba?" And then Akiba's story would be told. [Yoma 35b]

When Akiba went off to study he went to the academies of Eliezer ben Hyrcanus and Joshua ben Hananiah and he took his son along with him. Can you picture the scene? There down a dusty road walk father and son, hand in hand, equally ignorant, on the road to Torah. Savor the scene:

> Both he and his son went and sat down before the school-teacher and said to him: "Master, teach us the Torah." Rabbi Akiba took hold of the tablet by one end and his son by the other end, and on it the teacher wrote "alef, bet" which he learnt, "alef, taw" which he learnt, and then the Book of Leviticus which he also learnt. [cf. Supplement: Akiba #2]

You will notice that after the beginning student learned the alphabet, he began the Pentateuch not with Genesis, but with Leviticus, on the principle that the "pure" should be exposed to the pure. After mastering the Pentateuch, they went on to study Mishnah, and all the halakhot.

Akiba was not the student to listen in silence. There was always a question on his lips. "Why is *alef* so written? Why is *bet* so written? Why is this stated?" His questions gushed forth, and frequently Joshua and Eliezer had no answer. Eliezer could only explain this constant chipping away at minutiae in terms of a stonemason who sat on a mountain top and began chipping away the rock. When asked why he was doing this, the reply was: "I intend to uproot the mountain." When told that this was impossible, he simply persisted until the mountain was leveled.

"Akiba," declared Eliezer, "was that kind of scholar, and uprooter of mountains, pebble by pebble [*oker harim*]. This descriptive term down through the ages came to be used to describe the great scholar who would be called "Sinai and *oker barim,*" that is to say, he is like Mount Sinai and is as well an uprooter of mountains!

This, then, is a glimpse of Akiba as innovator, Akiba as a crucial link in the development of the chain of Rabbinic exegesis and of Jewish survival. He lived for the Torah that he helped to shape, and finally he died for it.

What about Akiba as martyr? He lived for the Torah and he died for the Torah. This involves a more careful look at the period between the destruction of Jerusalem and the founding of the center at Yavneh in the year 70, and the Bar Cochba Revolt, which began in the year 132 and ended in total disaster three years later.

Although we have thus far made the year 70, the year of the destruction of the Temple, as the watershed year, from which Rabbinic Judaism on the one hand and early Christianity on the other take over as surviving branches, it did not mark the end of the Roman-Jewish War.

The year 70 was merely the end of phase one. What Johanan ben Zakkai and the Men of Yavneh did was to win a respite. Their non-aggression agreement with the Romans did not mean their acceptance of Roman rule or of total submission. Everything they did leading to survival was really an act of resistance. The sages were simply careful not to overstep the boundary that might bring utter destruction.

However, resistance continued. During the reign of Trajan, revolt broke out in the rest of the Empire, outside of the Land of Israel where Jews resided in great numbers. In Cyrenaica, in Libya, in Alexandria revolt erupted. This is not reported in Jewish sources, and not in Josephus. However the Roman historian Dio Cassius deals with it. He vividly describes the revolt breaking out under the leadership of a certain Andreas. According to his report, hundreds of thousands perished, and atrocities were committed. The revolt was finally put down by a general, Lusius, who was sent by Trajan to crush the uprising.

These events are also recorded in writings of contemporary Church Fathers. What we are seeing here is another instant messianic outbreak, reflecting a refusal to accept defeat.

In the Land of Israel, the revolt broke out when the Emperor Hadrian decided to build a shrine to Jupiter on the site of the Temple. It was a carefully prepared revolt, as recent excavations have shown, and as Dio himself reports. He could write, for example:

> This brought on a war of no slight importance nor of brief duration, for the Jews deemed it intolerable that foreign races should be settled in their city and foreign religious rites be planted here. So long, indeed, as Hadrian was close by in Egypt and again in Syria, they remained quiet, save in so far as they purposely made of poor quality such weapons as they were called upon to furnish, in order that the Romans might reject them and they themselves thus have the use of them; but when they went further away, they openly revolted. [Cassius Dio, Roman Histories, LXIX, Loeb Classical Library]

Thus he introduces the Revolt of Bar Cochba, whom he does not name. He describes how Hadrian found it necessary to send his best General, Severus, recalling him from Britain to put down the revolt. Dio describes a brutal extermination, the destruction of fifty outposts, of nine hundred and fifty villages, and five hundred and eighty thousand slain, "and the number of those that perished by famine, disease and fire was past finding out." Dio adds that it was a very costly war for the Romans.

The Bar Cochba revolt represented the last bid the Jewish nation made for freedom in two thousand years. It marked the beginning of the end of mass Jewish settlement in their home. The center of Jewish population moved northward to Galilee, and in the wake of the ruins, that task begun by the Pharisee/Rabbinic/Sages was completed and moved to Babylonia.

This disaster is echoed in fragmentary sources both in the Talmud and the Midrash, and there is some ambivalence as to whether Bar Cochba was really the Messiah. This from Lamentations Rabbah 2:4 by way of example:

> When Rabbi Akiba beheld Bar Kosiba he exclaimed:
> "This is the king Messiah!" Rabbi Johanan ben Torta
> retorted: "Akiba, grass will grow in your cheeks and he
> will still not have come!"

But there is no ambivalence about the horror and impact of the
event, and the scattered accounts of the imprisonment and death
of Akiba and the way in which his death is remembered underscore for us, without a shadow of doubt, Akiba's role as the
martyr, whose martyrdom and heroism was deeply etched upon
the consciousness of the Jewish people.

These passages, taken together from their disparate sources
and read together, have an impact on the reader matched only
by Plato's moving account of the death of Socrates. And reflecting on the parallel, we can see clearly and sharply how the Rabbinic and Greco-Roman method differed in how central events
were recorded.

The Greeks were systematic, structured, organized. Hence,
the account of the intellectual leaders of the Stoa, as recorded by
Plato, giving us the image of that extraordinary Socrates, emerges
in his unforgettable dialogues.

A reading of the Crito and Phaedo, together with selected
passages about the imprisonment and death of Akiba, makes the
point. The former has a sense of unity and completeness, as it
describes the sentencing, imprisonment and last days of Socrates
in prison. Here he is surrounded by his disciples, who are in
discussion with him on central issues to the very end. The action
mounts to a moving crescendo.

The Akiba story was never written in this way. It survived in
a variety of traditions and a variety of memories. But when you
bring them together, and that is what must be done to have a
coherent view of the rabbinic tradition, its impact is just as great,
and just as moving—perhaps even more so.

As the Bar Cochba revolt raged, the government imposed
stronger and stronger sanctions. It forbade the rite of circumcision. It forbade the studying of Torah. It forbade the teaching of
Torah. Ultimately the greatest of the teaching sages perished,
Akiba the first among them.

As the net closed in, Akiba kept on teaching. When cautioned by a Jewish supporter of Rome, Pappus ben Judah, to refrain from doing this, Akiba's reply was a sharp no and the parable of the fox, who saw fish scurrying around in the river, fleeing from the nets of men. "Why not come up to me on dry land and I will protect you," the fox suggested. To which the fish replied, "You are really foolish and not wise, for if we are in danger in our natural environment, how much more so on dry land?" And he concluded:

> So it is with us. If such is our condition when we sit and study Torah, of which it is written: "For that is thy life and the length of thy days," if we go and neglect it how much worse off shall we be? [cf. Supplement: Akiba #18]

So he was imprisoned. And Pappus soon joined him. He too was caught in the net and could only say to Akiba: "You were arrested for something important, and I for trivialities."

It was the local governor, Tinneius Rufus, who imprisoned him and finally ordered his execution, but a number of episodes describe a dialogue between the two—I should say, the three, for it included his wife. The discussions included a wide range of subjects, the value of the Sabbath, why circumcision, the tension between Jacob and Esau, God's justice [and injustice]. In general its range included the issues debated between Jews and Pagans and Jews and early Christians. The give and take is sharp and incisive, not in the calm reflective mood of the Socratic dialogues with his disciples.

While in prison, we have evidence that Akiba's disciples made their way to him—sometimes, with the permission of the jailers, entering his cell, and in other cases by stratagem. In one instance, one of his disciples, Judah the shoemaker, who needed confirmation of a decision he had made in a matter of law, disguised himself as a peddler and

> passed by the prison where Rabbi Akiba was incarcerated, crying out: "Who wants to buy needles? Who

wants to buy needles? Can levirate marriage be nullified
without witnesses? Who wants to buy needles?" Rabbi
Akiba came to the window and said: "Do you have flax?
Do you have wool? Your decision is valid." [cf. Supplement: Akiba #12]]

On another occasion, another disciple, Simeon bar Yohai,
came to him in prison and asked him to teach him Torah. And
we are informed that Akiba informed him that he wanted to
teach more than the disciple wanted to learn. As he put it: "More
than the calf wishes to suck does the cow desire to suckle!" [cf.
Supplement: Akiba #10] We learn that Akiba was able to intercalate a leap year from prison on request from his students.

When he was in prison, another of his disciples, Rabbi Judah the Gritsmaker was attending on him. One day, without
warning, the supply of water for Akiba was sharply reduced by
the jailer. When left with a choice of either drinking the water or
washing his hands to perform a commandment, he chose the
latter course with the words:

> "What can I do, when for neglecting the words of the
> Sages one deserves death? It is better that I myself
> should die than that I should transgress against the
> opinion of my colleagues." It was related that he tasted
> nothing until the other brought him water wherewith to
> wash his hands. [cf. Supplement: Akiba #11]

When the Sages heard of this they were moved to remark in
wonder that "if he was so scrupulous in his old age, how much
more must he have been in his youth; and if he so behaved in
prison, how much more [would he have behaved thus] when
free." I cannot help but think of Socrates, before he drinks the
poison, taking his bath, and then seeing his children to say farewell to them! And the description of his end—who can forget it?

> As he [the executioner] spoke, he handed the cup to
> Socrates, who received it quite cheerfully . . . and said
> looking up under his brows with his usual steady gaze:

"What do you say about pouring a libation from this drink? Is it permitted or not?" Up till then most of us had been fairly successful in keeping back our tears, but when we saw that he was drinking . . . we could no longer do so. [Phaedo, p. 97, Plato's Dialogues, Bollingen Edn., 1969]

And with his last words to Crito: "Crito, we ought to offer a cock to Asclepius. See to it and don't forget," he dies.

Thus one great culture remembers its great culture hero. The last days of Akiba are just as moving, perhaps more so, in this same sense. Not perhaps with the cumulative power of the Plato narrative, because the memories are scattered, though preserved in the Jewish way. Let the words speak for themselves:

When Akiba was taken out for execution, it was the hour for the recital of the *Shma,* and while they combed his flesh with iron combs, he was accepting upon himself the kingship of heaven. His disciples said to him: "Our teacher, even to this point?" He said to them: "All my days I have been troubled with the verse [in the Shma] 'with all thy soul,' [which I interpret] 'even if He takes thy soul.' I said: 'When shall I have the opportunity of fulfilling this? Now that I have the opportunity, shall I not fulfill it?' " He prolonged the word *ehad* until he expired while saying it. [cf. Supplement: Akiba #18]

Akiba was the first of the ten leading scholars to die a martyr's death, along with tens of thousands of disciples, and hundreds of thousands of the people. But what had been wrought, what they shaped, had ensured survival. Its years in the Land of Israel were numbered. The generation or two that followed provided a respite for Judah the Prince to complete the work of Akiba and his colleagues, and to see the national treasure, Scripture, Mishnah, Jerusalem Talmud and Prayer Book, move to a thriving center in Babylonia.

Before his death Akiba and his colleagues, who were soon to follow him in death, secretly ordained new rabbinic leaders, and at Usha the last group was ordained by Judah ben Baba, who then interposed himself between the disciples and the Roman soldiers, throwing his body to them, to delay them, as the escape was completed. Here is how it is recorded:

> Once the wicked government decreed that whoever performed ordination should be put to death and whoever received ordination should be put to death, and the city in which ordination took place, demolished. What did Judah ben Baba do? He went and sat between two great mountains [that lay] between two large cities between Usha and Shefaram, and there ordained five elders. . . . As soon as their enemies discovered them, he urged them: "My children, flee." They said to him: "What will become of you, Rabbi?" "I lie before them like a stone which none [is concerned] to overthrow," he replied. It is said that the enemy did not stir from the spot until they had driven three hundred iron spear-heads into his body. [Sanhedrin 14a]

It is interesting to note that the brutal, extermination-type repression directed at the Jewish people in the aftermath of the Bar Cochba Revolt in 135 was directed at Christians twenty years later. One of the Christian victims was Justin Martyr, a Greek born in Shechem, who knew Jews, Judaism and probably Hebrew, and whose path may well have crossed Akiba's!

What a firm and sturdy root, though tender and vulnerable flower, is the Pharisaic/Rabbinic process that shaped Jewish survival. We have watched it grow from episode after episode of near extinction, always in the aftermath of the disaster of a national defeat.

Even though the completion of the work is credited to Judah the Prince, so that the Mishnah is associated with his name, as the English Bible is associated with the name King James, it is Akiba and his disciples who bring it to fruition and fulfillment. The Rabbinic exegetic process has been fully developed and fully shaped. The leadership core is in place, bloodied but unbowed. The task of communicating to the people must go forward.

Chapter Eight

Meir and Elisha ben Abuya

It has become apparent by this time that Rabbinic Judaism is characterized at one and the same time by continuity and dialectic. This is apparent as we encounter Meir, a disciple and successor to Akiba. Herein lies the continuity. His other teacher was Elisha ben Abuya, and herein lies the dialectic. Meir carried forward his work beyond the trauma of the indescribable pain of the Bar Cochba wars and the Hadrianic persecution. Elisha, on the other hand, could not accept the possibility that God could have permitted such suffering. He rejected Judaism, turned his back upon his people, and moved over to the pagan world.

The one carried forward the classification process begun by Akiba, and that culminated with the Mishnah as edited by Judah the Prince. The other decided that the Jewish people must disappear, because a God responsible for such injustice did not deserve to have a covenant people bear eternal witness to His being. It is in fact surmised that it was he who suggested the pattern for destroying the Jew by destroying its teachers and the Study of Torah, in order to assure this result!

The two of them, Meir and Elisha ben Abuya, were the closest of friends. And poignantly, their friendship survived Elisha's abrupt break with Judaism. It is an example of the dialectic process within Rabbinic Judaism taken to its extreme. It is perhaps a dialectic as well that helps us understand the painful relationship between Judaism and Christianity for almost two millennia, and to understand the inner core of communication that has made possible the kind of fruitful and potentially healing dialogue that is going on in our time.

Meir, in addition to playing a key role in the development of the exegetical process in Rabbinic Judaism, was one of the most gifted popular preachers, or darshanim, of his time, and creates for us an appropriate bridge for the shift from our account of how rabbinic exegesis developed, to a glimpse into the story of Jewish preaching, and the development of the sermon, which is central to the development of Christianity as well as of Rabbinic Judaism.

That Rabbi Meir was concerned as a fitting successor to Akiba is clear from Rabbinic tradition. As promoters of the idea that Oral Law, of which they were both guardian and transmitter, was coequal with the Written Law, it was in their interest to make later generations of sages as important as their predecessors. Hence the Akiba/Moses tradition, which has already been noted.

There is a similar tradition about Meir. Commenting on the verse from the Song of Songs: "New and old have I laid up for Thee, O my beloved" [S/S 7:14], the midrashic homilist deduced that the "old ones" referred to Abraham, Isaac and Jacob, and the "new ones" to the generation of Moses. Here is a clear affirmation of the transition from the patriarchal age to the beginning of the First Commonwealth, and the affirmation of the principle of change. Abraham would have reacted to Moses as Moses had reacted to Akiba.

Then the passage continues, with an alternative suggestion:

> The company of Moses, the company of Joshua, the company of David and Hezekiah are meant by "old ones," whilst the companies of Ezra, Hillel, Rav Johanan ben Zakkai and Reb Meir are meant by "new ones."
> [Supplement: Meir #2]

Akiba has been displaced by Meir! Does this suggest a diminution of the importance of Akiba? Not at all. It simply underscores the attitude of Rabbinic Judaism to constructive change with emphasis on the importance of those who shape that change! Meir is clear successor to Akiba.

Meir functioned in the post-Bar Cochba and post-Usha period. The consolidation of what had been achieved up to that time, from Yavneh to his day, living as they did on the edge of destruction and the edge of survival all at once, made this a crucial necessity, and Meir was the man for the task.

If we find the importance in which he was held by subsequent generations underscored in one text, we find the reason for it in another. It is recorded [Berakhot 63a] that Sages, during the latter days of the Hadrianic War and persecutions, came across Meir's colleagues writing down *halakhot* on the Sabbath! Horrified by what they saw, they taxed them for this serious violation. They countered with a radical interpretation of the verse from the Psalms [119:126]:

> It is time to act for the Lord for they are violating Your teachings.

It is possible to read the Hebrew text in such a way as to replace the word "for" with the word "by."

Sometimes it is necessary to act for the Lord *by* violating His commandments, it was suggested. In such times of crisis, it was more important to save the Torah than to observe the ban on writing on the Sabbath. This is what preserving the Oral Law by making possible the Mishnah is precisely what Meir did, and his act of vision and of heroism was thus remembered and recorded.

Meir was exegete par excellence. He himself related:

> When I was with Rabbi Akiba, I used to put vitriol into my ink and he told me nothing against it, but when I subsequently came to Rabbi Ishmael, the latter said to me: "What is your occupation?" I told him: "I am a scribe," and he said to me: "Be meticulous in your work, for your occupation is a sacred one." [Supplement: Meir #4]

His marginal notes and his glosses were very instructive. In the Tractate Ta'anit of the Jerusalem Talmud we read that "in Meir's copy of Isaiah [21:11] they found it written: 'Massa Duma should be read Massa Roma.' " The intensity of his feelings about Rome as oppressing power come through clearly and with great force.

Along these lines, his gloss to Genesis 1:30 is instructive. When at the end of the sixth day, God sees that what He had done was "very good" [*tov m'od*], Meir wrote in the Torah which he copied: "Read it rather '*tov mot*'—death is good!" Have we not here a reflection on the rampant death and martyrdom which was being experienced, and was this perhaps not a validation of martyrdom, and a view of death that marked the end of the struggle against the evil impulse, and that achievement of ultimate peace? How differently Elisha ben Abuya viewed this, we shall subsequently see.

The very way in which this is recalled underscores not only Meir's profound insight, but there is an echo of the impact that he left upon the folk memory as a preacher. Listen to how a man who became a great darshan in his time remembers:

> Rabbi Samuel bar Nahmani said: "I was seated on my grandfather's shoulder going up from my town to Kfar Hana via Beit She'an, and I heard Rabbi Simeon ben Eleazer say in Rabbi Meir's name: 'And behold it was very good, behold death is very good.'" [Supplement: Meir #12]

Thus did his preaching powers pass down through the generations and become indelibly impressed upon the memory of a child.

There is an even more poignant episode, and it relates that so powerful a preacher was he that his eloquence almost broke up a marriage and his wisdom and tact saved it.

When Meir was not giving leadership to halakhic interpretation in the highest councils of the Sanhedrin he spent much of his time instructing the ordinary folk through his lectures and sermons. This he tended to do on Sabbath evenings. Great crowds of men and women came to listen to him.

There was a certain housewife who came every week to listen to him. One time, his sermon was longer than usual, and she got home too late to prepare her husband's dinner. Her husband was furious:

"Where have you been?" he asked her. She answered: "I was sitting listening to the voice of the preacher." Said he to her: "I swear I will not let you enter here until you go and spit in the face of the preacher." [Supplement: Meir #13]

Somehow Meir heard what had happened. At his next lecture, seeing her present [presumably for her the preacher came first!], he said: "Is there a woman among you clever at whispering a charm over an eye?" Her neighbor urged her to go forward, and she did. Shyly she said that she did not believe she knew the formula, to which Meir replied: "Just spit in my eye seven times and I will be cured." And she did, and could then return home. To create peace between husband and wife was the highest level of a good deed, and it was characteristic of Meir to do just that!

Meir was a man of great tolerance, unusual for his time. He had many contacts with the outside world. He was a close friend of Oenomaus of Gadara, a pagan philosopher of the school of the younger cynics. Though his works have virtually disappeared, excerpts of them have been preserved by Eusebius, the well known early historian of Christianity. He appears in Rabbinic literature as Avinomos haGeradi, and was well-disposed to Jews and Judaism.

One conversation between him and Meir, recorded in Hagigah 15b of the Babylonian Talmud, appears to refer to Meir's teacher, Elisha, who had become an apostate. Oenomos is quoted as asking Meir: "Does all wool rise that is placed in the dyeing pot?" To which Meir replied: "What was clean upon the body of the mother rises, what was unclean upon the body of the mother does not rise."

This enigmatic exchange suggested that he was asking Meir why he continued to study with Elisha after his apostasy, and Meir's reply was that there was still something to learn from him! In another instance, commenting on a Rabbinic observation that a *mamzer* [a Jew of dubious ancestry] who is a scholar in Torah outranks a High Priest who is an ignoramus, Meir goes a step further to say that even a gentile who studies Torah out-ranks a High Priest who is an ignoramus. He used to say:

> Whence do we know that even an idolator who studies the Torah is equal to a High Priest? From the following verse: *You shall keep my laws and rules, by the pursuit of which man shall live.* It does not say priest or Israelite, but *man.* Here then you can learn that even a heathen who studies Torah is equal to a High Priest! [Supplement: Meir #14]

Meir was fluent in Latin and Greek, familiar with the literature and culture, and was known as a master of Latin and Greek animal fables. It is not surprising, therefore, that he maintained contact with his teacher after his apostasy.

What could the reason be for such a breadth of view in a society that in its herculean efforts to survive found it necessary to be separatist and exclusive? It is not easy to surmise. There was a tradition that Meir was descended from a convert. This is not an unusual tradition, for we already know that the teachers of Hillel, Shemaiah and Abtalion, were both believed to have been descended from Sisera, and Hillel was described as a prose-lyte from Babylonia.

The tradition about Meir comes from a long series of legendary/historical accounts of the last days of Jerusalem. Here is how it reads:

> He [the Emperor] sent against them Nero the Caesar. As he was coming he shot an arrow towards the east, and it fell in Jerusalem. He then shot one toward the west, and it again fell in Jerusalem. He shot toward all four points of the compass, and each time it fell in Jerusalem. He said to a certain boy: Repeat to me the last verse of scripture which you learnt. He said: "And I will lay my hand in vengeance upon Edom by the hand of my people Israel." [Ezekiel 24:5]. He said: The Holy One Praised be He desires to lay waste his house and lay the blame on me. So he ran away and became a prose-

lyte, and Rabbi Meir was descended from him. [Supplement: Meir #11]

This is clearly not factual, since Nero never came to the Land of Israel and was overthrown while Vespasian was besieging Jerusalem. That Meir was really a descendant of Nero's might well be contested as too fanciful. That he was descended from a proselyte is a clearly accepted tradition. Giving this extraordinary human being such an ancestor has within it a touch of irony spiced with humor. But who ever accused the Sages of being humorless, straight-laced folk!

Meir's last years were filled with pain and tragedy. His two sons, brilliant and full of promise, died suddenly, on a Sabbath, while he was in the house of study, preaching. His wife, Beruriah, daughter of the martyred Haninah ben Teradion, and in her own right a scholar and intellectual, one of the most brilliant and accomplished women in Rabbinic record, had to break the news to him as he came home.

The account is told with an amazing degree of sensitivity. It is related that as was his custom, Meir was sitting and expounding in the synagogue, and while he was there, his two sons died. The mother first placed the two of them on a bed, and awaited her husband's return.

She did not burst out with the news as he entered, but first served him his evening meal. When he asked for his two sons, because he had missed them in the synagogue, she gave him an evasive answer. When he was finished she said to him: "May I ask you a question?" "Ask," he replied. What was she to do, she continued, if someone left a pledge with her and she was called upon to return it? "My beloved," he replied, "is not he who holds a pledge required to return it to its rightful owner?" "If it were not for your opinion," she then said, "I would not have returned it." Then

she took him by the hand, led him to the room and brought him right up to his bed. She lifted up the sheet and uncovered them, and he beheld his two sons dead on the bed. He began to weep and cry: "My sons! My

sons! My teachers! My teachers! My sons in the way of
the world, and my teachers who brightened my eyes
with their Torah!" At that moment she said to him:
"Master, did you not say yourself that we must return
the pledge to the owner? The Lord has given, the Lord
has taken away, blessed be the name of the Lord." [Sup-
plement: Meir #1]

This was, for him, probably the most painful. But there
were others—there were the painful events around the time of
the Bar Cochba Revolt and the Hadrianic persecutions. The
massacres, especially the massacres and martyr deaths of the
Sages, among them his first teacher Akiba, touched him deeply.
Even closer to home was the flaming death endured by his
saintly father-in-law, Hanina ben Teradyon, who perished in
flames with a Torah Scroll wrapped around him. Hanina had
fathered Beruriah, one of the most gifted and brilliant women of
her time, the model par excellence for Jewish feminists in our
day. It was said of Beruriah that she had learned three hundred
halakhot from three hundred teachers in three hours!

Brilliance was linked to sensitivity, as we have seen, and to
brilliance and sensitivity were linked pain. Not only did Beruriah
and Meir experience this pain, but they also saw her sister carried off to a brothel in Rome, and the tradition has it that Meir
journeyed to Rome with a bagful of denarii to bribe the jailer.

In this connection we get a bizarre story, but it is worth
retelling. Disguised as a Roman knight [to picture Meir in a toga
blows my mind] he enters the brothel and asks for Beruriah's
sister. She pretends she is not well. When he tells her he will wait,
she suggests other more beautiful maidens. Meir now realizes
that her virtue is intact, and he offers the bribe. "What," says the
jailer, "do I do when the money runs out?" Replies Meir: "Just
say: The God of Meir help me." The dubious jailer asks for
proof. Just then he is attacked by a dog, he cries out the suggested formula, and he is saved. So the bribe is completed, and
the damsel in distress is rescued.

And then of course there was the tragedy and pain of the
apostasy of his beloved teacher Elisha ben Abuya.

You may recall how, earlier in this book, there was a reference to four options in the Jewish reaction to the destruction of Jerusalem and the exile, fight to the death, retreat to resist better; withdrawal from the world, and going over to the other side. We mentioned the nephew of Philo, who was second in command to Titus. We mentioned El'azar ben Arakh who went to Emmaus and forgot his Torah. And now we meet Elisha ben Abuya, who does not forget his Torah, but who defects to the other side, and is thereafter known as Aher—the Other One, the unmentionable, the un-nameable.

Aher went over to the other side not out of fear, but out of the deepest conviction. He could not accept the injustice which he saw in the theodicy—God's injustice, as it appeared to him, was more than could be borne.

The problem of evil and of what appears to be God's injustice has always tended to overwhelm humanity. The book of Job is evidence of this. Job confronts God with the problem of the suffering of the righteous, and God answers him in a whirlwind. Jeremiah cries out to God, *"Why are wicked rewarded while the righteous suffer?"* And he receives the reply: *"You have run against men and you are tired; how will you do against horses? And if you stumble in comfortable terrain, how will you do in the jungle of the Jordan?"* And Abraham could cry out in wonder, aghast that the righteous would suffer with the wicked at Sodom: "Will the Judge of all the earth do injustice?"

In each instance, their faith survives their questions. But the questions remain. Echoes of the cry of protest are in the Talmudic records. Here and there we find poignant echoes of this. In looking at the horror of the destruction of the Temple, the silence of God seemed incomprehensible and intolerable. The interpretation of the lines "Who is like Thee among the mighty, O God" [mi kamokha *ba-elim* Adonay] to be read as "Who is like Thee among the silent, O God" [mi kamokha *ba-ilmim* Adonay] echoes this anguished feeling.

So does a midrash by Samuel bar Nahmani the sage who as a child was sitting on his grandfather's shoulders when he heard Rabbi Meir make his comment that "tov m'od" [very good] should be read as "tov mot" [death is good]. He gives a very moving account of how all the greats of the Jewish people, Abraham, Isaac, Jacob, Moses, and Jeremiah, came, one after another, to plead with God to spare the Temple and Jerusalem. Each one is turned down. Finally Rachel throws herself at God's feet, reminds God how willingly she cooperated with her father in the deception of Jacob about Leah, how she hid in the marriage chamber, speaking for Leah, and finally crying out: "O God, if I, just flesh and blood, could contain my anger and jealousy, you, Ruler of the world, can you not contain your anger?" At which, Samuel bar Nahmani continued: "God wept and said: Rachel, I can do nothing now. But when the time comes, the redemption will be for your sake!" [Lamentations Rabbah, Proem #24] Here we have the image of a God of limited power, the only way, perhaps, the sages could come to terms with the theodicy.

Finally, there is a postscript to the Moses/Akiba story. When Moses saw how brilliant Akiba was, he said to God: "You have shown me a great scholar. Now show me his end." So God showed him Akiba being flayed alive. "This is the Torah and this is its reward?" asks Moses with incredulous anger, knowing that this is even worse than his not entering the Promised Land. "Be silent! That's the way it must be," God answers.

When you do not have a proper answer, you become angry. Here is another subtle example of this Rabbinic attitude. There are those who experienced God's silence at Auschwitz, and would not accept it.

Such a one was Elisha ben Abuya. Rabbinic tradition is of two minds about him. Some sources are hostile. Elisha ben Abuya was one of the four who "entered Pardes," that is to say, achieved a mystical vision of the divine, and "cut the roots." As the tradition has it:

> Four men entered the "garden," namely, Ben Azzai, Ben Zoma, Aher and Akiba. . . . Ben Azzai cast a look and died. . . . Ben Zoma looked and became demented. . . . Aher mutilated the shoots. Rabbi Akiba departed unhurt. [Supplement: Akiba #5]

This version suggests that he was incapable of handling the mystical revelation of the divine. One tradition suggests that he saw the Angel Metatron seated next to God, and concluded from this the ultimate heresy, that is the dualist, gnostic heresy suggesting that there were two Gods.

There are traditions that suggest that he was violent and vicious in his efforts to lead students in the academies away from Torah. One such source suggests that he would go from school to school and say to one: "Why study Torah? Become a carpenter." To others he would suggest such occupations as tailor, hunter, tanner. Anything but scholar, anything but sage.

One source went so far to suggest that he could be very vicious. It is related that at one of the times that R. Meir was trying to get him to repent, he took him to a schoolhouse where children were studying. Elisha stopped one student after another, to ask them what new verse they had studied. Each one, one after another, cited a verse which pointed to Elisha's apostasy. Then finally:

> He took him to yet another schoolhouse . . . all of them quoted in a similar vein. When he said to the last one, Recite for me thy verse, he answered: "But unto the wicked [laresha'im] God saith: 'What hast thou to do to declare my statutes?' " That child was a stutterer, so it sounded as though he answered: "But to Elisha God saith." Some say that Aher had a knife with him, and he cut him up and sent him to thirteen schools. And some say: Had I a knife in my hand, I would have cut him up. [Hagiga 15b]

Hardly a gentle man, if we accept this passage at its face value. In another instance, there is a passage in Berakot which deals with the significance of dreams. For instance:

> If one sees an elephant in a dream, a miracle will be wrought for him. . . . If one sees wheat in a dream it

> suggests peace. . . . If one sees vines laden with grapes, one's wife will bear healthy children. . . .

And then we encounter this:

> If one sees Ben Azzai in a dream, he may hope for piety; if Ben Zoma, he may hope for wisdom; if Aher, let him fear for punishment.

Then there are those who see a more understandable reason for his defection. It comes out in a Talmudic discussion that touches very closely on the idea of God's justice. In the Torah there is the interesting command that if you want to take the eggs of a bird from the nest, you must first send the mother away. For this, the reward is the same as honoring parents, i.e., long life.

In connection with this the story is told of a grandfather who sent his grandson up a ladder to perform this commandment, and the child fell and was killed. The question then is, "What kind of long life is this?" Rabbi Jacob replies that "your life shall be long" must be taken to refer to the world to come.

As a follow-up to this lengthy discussion we read:

> Rabbi Joseph said: Had Aher interpreted this verse as Rabbi Jacob, his daughter's son, did, he would not have sinned. What actually did he see?—Some say he saw such an occurrence. Others say, He saw the tongue of R. Huzpith the Interpreter lying on a dungheap, and he exclaimed, "Shall the mouth that uttered pearls lick the dust?" [Hullin 142a]

You see, a great deal of empathy, sympathy and understanding comes out of this passage. To be sure, the one who gives the interpretation that defends God's integrity is given by Aher's grandson. But I am inclined to suspect that empathy for Aher's feelings was there. Clearly defense lay behind the explanation.

Because of the rupture, and despite the face that Elisha was such an outstanding scholar of Torah, there are relatively few references to him in the Talmud. A look at the index of Rabbinic sages in the Soncino translation of the Babylonian Talmud will show hundreds of citations of Rabbi Akiba, and hundreds of Meir, but just a handful of Elisha ben Abuya.

We have already noted the reasons given for his defection. How did he do it? This is what we read:

> He went forth, found a harlot and demanded her. She said to him: Are you not Elisha ben Abuya? But when he tore a radish out of its bed on the Sabbath and gave it to her, she said: It is another—Aher. [Hagiga 15a]

Just a few lines previously, his offense was described as "mutilating the shoots"—here it becomes a plucked up radish on the Sabbath.

Ah that radish. Once this passage helped me understand a lithograph by an Israeli artist that hangs in our house. It is a striking picture by Yossi Bergner, dominated by a somber, grey, Jerusalem stone, Turkish mansion, with a free floating bright red radish hovering over it like a Magritte painting.

We liked the picture for its color contrast—and the floating radish was particularly attractive. But we never understood what the picture was about. It happened one day that I was working on Elisha ben Abuya material from the Talmud, and sitting at the desk before the wall where this picture had been hung, I read and reflected upon this passage. As I read it, and thought about it, I looked up at the picture. There it was, clear as a flash. Elisha ben Abuya's radish, and the gray somber house. The artist had captured that moment of revolt, of rejection, of release. The picture and its text had met!

We come back to the relationship between Meir and Aher, that Other One. The shaper of Judaism's future will not break with his apostate teacher who would destroy it. Strange how both operated out of the same motive, love of the Jewish people, but operated in opposite directions. Deep down was the issue whether or not God in punishing the Jewish people had gone too far. Both were probably not too far apart on that. Their difference was on the dimension of faith.

The encounters between Meir and Elisha have two versions, one in the Babylonian Talmud, and one in the Jerusalem Talmud. They are substantially the same, showing how Meir learned Torah from Elisha after his apostasy, and how he kept trying to win his return.

There are two crucial differences in the two versions. The latter has an illuminating account of Elisha's youth, and it has a much more compassionate and understanding account of his death. This difference is very illuminating. The Jerusalem Talmud was completed closer to the events recorded. The account in the Babylonian Talmud was a century or two later. The fact that the earlier account was more sympathetic than the latter is very instructive. There was more understanding of and sympathy for Elisha in the tradition closer to the event.

In any event, the Jerusalem Talmud version in Hagiga represents Elisha as telling Meir the following account of his childhood:

> My father Abuya was one of the most prominent citizens of Jerusalem. On the day of my circumcision, he invited all the important people of the town to the celebration, and set aside a house for them. He also arranged special quarters for Rabbis Joshua and Eliezer. After the ceremony and the meal, the guests began to dance and play games. Eliezer and Joshua said: Let us occupy ourselves in another way. Let us study Torah. . . . [Jerusalem Talmud, Hagiga II:1]

The story goes on to relate that as they studied, a fire descended from heaven and surrounded them. Smelling smoke, Abuya rushed in from the dancing and carousing and cried out to them: "What are you trying to do, burn my house down?" They reassured him and explained to him that their study was so intense that it was the fire of Mount Sinai that surrounded them.

Mollified, Abuya said: "In that case, I promise to dedicate my son to the study of Torah." Which, said Elisha, he did, but he did it out of selfish reasons and not for its own sake, and he added: That is why it did not succeed in the end.

The pathos and deep sense of regret, coupled with a conviction that there was no way back, comes through clearly.

Meir and Elisha must have dialogued often, but the dialogue that has come down to us took place on the Sabbath, with Elisha riding on his horse [publicly desecrating the Sabbath] and Meir following him, discussing Torah with him and trying to persuade him to repent. Nay more, we are told that Meir was in the synagogue that Saturday afternoon teaching and preaching when he heard Elisha come by. He left his teaching and preaching to walk with Elisha.

What did they talk about? Elisha would ask Meir how he interpreted a scriptural text. Meir would give his interpretation, and in each instance Elisha would say that he had a different tradition about the verse from Akiba.

For example, he asked Meir about the verse from Ecclesiastes [7:14]: "God hath made even the one as the other." Meir responded that this meant that God created a counterpart for everything He created—first mountains and hills and then seas and rivers. "No," retorted Aher, "Rabbi Akiba thy master did not explain it thus, but as follows: He created righteous and he created wicked. He created the Garden of Eden and he created Gehinnom."

On another occasion he asked Meir about the meaning of the verse: "Gold and glass cannot equal it; neither shall the exchange thereof be vessels of fine gold." [Job 28:17] Rabbi Meir took this to mean that the words of the Torah which are hard to acquire, like vessels of gold, are easily destroyed like vessels of glass. "No," replied Aher.

> Rabbi Akiba thy master did not explain it thus, but as follows: Just as vessels of gold and vessels of glass have a remedy, even so a scholar who has sinned has a remedy. [Hag. 15a]

Thereupon Meir said to him: "Then thou too repent!" To which he replied, "It is too late. I heard from behind the veil that repentance is possible for everybody but Aher!"

Always the discussions on Scripture centered on Meir giving

one interpretation and Aher telling him what Akiba taught, with the thrust turning on his apostasy and the impossibility of repentance. And always Meir follows him and pleads with him to return.

In fact as Meir followed Aher and his horse on the Sabbath, they reached the limit of the distance an observant Jew could walk on the Sabbath, and Aher cautioned "Meir, you have come to the limit of what is permissible for the Sabbath. Turn back!" And Meir would retort: "You turn back too!" Just as the prophets had said that ultimately God would not abandon his people eternally, Meir would not abandon his teacher.

In Babylon they must have worried about this persistence of Meir's. Did not this tarnish his credibility. Dimi reassured them by saying: In the West [i.e. the Land of Israel] they say: R. Meir ate the date and threw the peel away. That is, he took the essence of the valued Torah teaching from the heretic, without himself being corrupted!

Did Aher have remorse at the end? The Babylonian Talmud versions give no indication of this. But in the Jerusalem Talmud version it is different. At the end of the running dialogue account, which is substantially the same in both versions, we read as follows:

> Shortly thereafter, Elisha fell ill. They came to Meir and told him: "Your teacher is dying." So he went to visit him. "Will you not repent your heresy?" "Will such repentance be accepted in Heaven?" asked Elisha. "Certainly", replied Meir; "even at the last moment repentance is accepted." Thereupon Elisha began to weep, and weeping, he died. [J. Hagiga II:1]*

At this juncture, we are told, Meir went away rejoicing, convinced that Elisha had in fact repented.

We can never know for sure. What we can know from how the traditions have come down to us, from the fact that the relationship between Meir and Elisha is preserved, is that there was not unqualified disapproval of Elisha's defection, that the pain of what he felt about the *deus absconditus,* the absent God, was felt even by sages who continued in their faith despite the unanswered Jobean questions.

When we think back on Simeon ben Shetah, Hillel, Johanan ben Zakkai, Eliezer and Joshua, Akiba, Meir and Elisha ben Abuya, we see how the process of survival through creative change and indestructible faith worked best by inclusion more than by exclusion, by dialectic more than by monolithic agreement. The differences between Hillel and Shammai and between Abaya and Rava, and even between believer and heretic, were all a crucial part of the mortar that held the structure together.

Chapter Nine

From Prophet to Preacher

We have thus far examined Rabbinic Judaism as a revolutionary mutation that made possible the survival of Judaism and the Jewish people in wake of the destruction of their state and their dispersion. We have seen how the Rabbinic-Pharisaic-Scribe process developed this through the the idea of the Oral Law and through midrash.

We have looked at the stages of the development of the exegetical process, and at some of the central figures that shaped it. We have examined the academies as centers for this study in the training of continuing generations of sages.

We have seen how Rabbinic Judaism and early Christianity emerged from the same stream of development, each motivated by the messianic drive and a sense for covenant survival. We have seen how this process reached out to the people and won their adherence.

To conclude this phase of the survey, it may be useful to take a brief look at another important element in the survival process which will be dealt with in detail in another volume. This has to do with the means of communicating all these ideas and values to the people. It has to do with the *derashah,* the sermon.

The sermon is the child of midrash. It, too, was a Jewish invention. It was the means of taking the text and bringing it to the people.

Thus we can say that the sermon, as spoken word based on sacred text, and directed toward the education of the people, grows out of the same rabbinic process that we have been following in the first eight lectures, and it grows out of it in a very special way.

In a way, it can be said that the sermon and spoken word is at the very source and origins of the Jewish experience. Even God began His intervention in the universe with the spoken word. When God said: "Let there be light," it can be said that we have the first sermon with instant result.

To be sure, historians of the Jewish sermon, qua sermon, situate the earliest sermon in the Tannaitic period, and find at least one complete sermon, as such, so recorded. It is a sermon by Rabbi Eleazar ben Azaraiah, found in Hagigah 3a in the Babylonian Talmud.

However it is possible to suggest that Abraham, the first Jew, began his career with the spoken word. To be sure, the inference comes from an exegetical interpretation of the text, in a way that some scholars would never accept. It is my feeling that the Rabbinic interpreters of Scripture had such a feel for what really went on that their comments have a dependability on which we can count. For the most part they had the right "feel" for the context, and very often it is very useful to turn to them.

Nevertheless, when we are informed that after accepting God's command to leave his home and his native land, and to go to a land that God would show him, the text records that Abraham [then Abram] took with him his wife Sarah [then Sarai], his flocks, and "the souls which he had gotten in Harran."

That last phrase cries out for interpretation. What could it possibly mean? The sages interpreted it to mean the converts he had made to the One God he had newly discovered. And how did he convert them? By talking to them, of course! By preaching to them! Hence Abraham must have been the first darshan!

So the sages see Abraham as the first preacher. Then how about Moses? What is the Torah that Moses receives at Sinai if not one great "Sermon on the Mount"? What is it if not a roaring, fiery sermon that sets the Jewish people on its course of destiny? Moses, in this sense, is the darshan par excellence. This is apparent at the beginning of his career at Mount Sinai. It is apparent throughout his career. It is especially apparent at the end of his career in those two masterful sermons in the book of Deuteronomy, written in such limpid prose and soaring poetry. I refer of course to his great sermon that encompasses the whole

book, and that sermon-poem *Ha'azinu* at the conclusion, where
he calls heaven and earth to witness, as he outlines, for the last
time to his people, their story, their destiny, and their covenant
obligation.

Of this poem, an early midrash [Sifrei, to Deuteronomy 32]
says:

> Great is song, for it contains the present, the past and
> the future; things of this world and things of the world
> to come.

What we deal with here, of course, is prophetic speech. Its inspiration comes directly from God, and the prophet speaks the
word to the people. It is direct speech. It is not text centered and
text oriented. The prophet does not prepare his text. He is the
human vessel, divinely chosen, to project God's message to the
people. It is the Mount Sinai syndrome, continued throughout
the period of the first commonwealth.

As we speak of prophecy in relation to the development of
preaching and of the sermon, it is well to remember the root
meaning of the Hebrew word for prophet. The root meaning of
the word *navi* is "spokesman." Moses, as we know was a stam-
merer, and when he raised this objection with God with respect
to his role, his brother Aaron was assigned to be his spokesman,
and the term used is "navi." When we come to the "meturgeman," the first actual preacher a little later, we will see its first
echo in Aaron.

That, indeed, is how Rashi and Ibn Ezra describe him. The
Midrash to this Exodus passage tells us that Moses and Aaron
would go among the people in Egypt, teaching, instructing and
inspiring them. In fact, we are told that "they had scrolls from
which they entertained the people, in order to persuade them
that God would redeem them." [Exodus Rabbah 80:5] You may
shrug your shoulders at this imaginative leap into the future, but
the darshanic link is clear.

The power of the spoken word in this sense emerges clearly
throughout the Bible. A few examples will suffice. When Samuel, the seer-prophet, comes upon the scene to lead the people, it

is because "the word of God was rare in those days." It had dried up and disappeared, and now it was restored.

And when Solomon, the wisest man of his time, expounded his wisdom, and it was finally brought together in a book, that book was called "Kohelet." "Kohelet" means "preacher." It comes from the word "kahal" which means "community." Kohelet really means: community-communicator. Let us take a glance at a pertinent passage from the Midrash Kohelet:

> All the people would gather together in the presence of Solomon to listen to words of wisdom which God had placed in his heart. That is why he was called "Kohelet" because his words were spoken before the community [kahal]. [Midrash, Yalkut Shim'oni II, par. 965]

King David could also be seen as preacher, communicating with the harp through his Psalms. I can just see the modern folk singer with the guitar, speaking to the soul of the people through folk songs, speaking of their hopes, fears and aspirations. All the ingredients for the sermon-derasha-folk communication are there.

We return, however to the prophet and prophetic speech, for that is the central factor in the process of development. Prophetic speech provided the core and kernel, which the various forms of derashah presented. For the words of the prophets were words of insight. They were words of warning, of denunciation, of consolation. By and large the prophet is at odds with the people because he tells them what they do not wish to hear.

Who can forget Isaiah's denunciation of the selfishness and insensitivity of the people who followed their pleasures and forgot God's directions? Who can forget the intensity and power of Jeremiah's Temple sermon which ends with the traumatic prediction of the destruction of the Temple where he was speaking?

Who can forget the fight for social justice of Amos and his cry?

> Assuredly, because you impose a tax on the poor and exact from him a levy of grain, you have built houses of hewn stone, but you shall not live in them; you have

planted delightful vineyards, but you shall not drink their wine. [Amos 5:11]

Who can forget Micah's prescription for decent conduct, his "do justly, love mercy and walk humbly with thy God"? Who can forget Deutero-Isaiah's words of consolation, when, after the destruction and his pain, he could bind the wounds with his *"Nahamu, nahamu 'ammi,* comfort ye, comfort ye, my people"?

And who can forget those last words of Malachi, that Malachi who as we have already noted may be one with Ezra, bridge from prophet to rabbinic/pharisaic/sage?

Remember ye the law of Moses my servant, which I commanded to him in Horeb, for all Israel, with the statutes and judgments. [Malachi 3:22]

Prophecy ceases, but God can henceforth speak to the people through Torah. The task of finding what God's message is and communicating it to the people becomes the task of the sages. They train other sages by teaching them how to exegete and communicate love of Torah, and what it teaches, and how one must react when it is tested; their purpose is to teach all the people through derashah and sermon.

These words of Malachi mark a shift in the nature of the communication of God's way to the people. Up to now it has been through prophets, directly inspired by God. The prophets did not speak out of texts. They communicated what God commanded them to say. From Jeremiah we learn how painful this could be:

When your words were offered, I devoured them; your word brought me delight and joy. . . . Why must my pain be endless, my wound incurable. . . . [Jeremiah 15:16/18]

But painful or not, that is the way it was. With the destruction of the First Commonwealth, the sacking of the Temple and the exile of the people, something changed and changed drastically.

For this catastrophe marked the end of many things. But most of all, it marked the end of prophecy. This reality is preserved in the Talmudic dictum: "When the Temple was destroyed prophecy ceased." [Sanhedrin 11a] The Children of Israel had heard from God directly at Sinai, and for the next six hundred years the Word of God comes to them from the prophets. But now, with the destruction and the end of prophecy, they were another step removed. Henceforth the Divine Will would be mediated through the sacred texts, brought together and prepared for them by the sages, and mediated by the sages through the process of midrash.

Since ultimately the Jewish people were to be God's witness to the world, and the bearers of the covenant promise and heritage, the people needed to know, the people needed to be taught.

It is Ezra, and if we are to believe the Targum comment [and more about this presently] Malachi-become-Ezra, or prophet transformed into Scribe/Sage/Pharisee, who makes the crucial change. The Torah, hitherto in possession of the priests, and read infrequently to the people, is now to become part of their regular discipline. It is to be read to them regularly and interpreted to them. It is to be introduced into the liturgy.

The Babylonian Talmud records ten innovations credited to Ezra, and the first two, and clearly in their eyes the most important, have to do with this. Thus we read in Baba Kama, folio 82a:

> The following ten enactments were ordained by Ezra:
> that the Torah be read publicly in the Minha [afternoon] service on Sabbath; that the Torah be read [publicly] on Mondays and Thursdays; that Courts be held on Mondays and Thursdays. . . .

Every Sabbath a portion from the Pentateuch is to be read, and the same portion is to be read on Mondays and Thursdays at morning prayers. And why Mondays and Thursdays? Because that was when people came into the market, so before they gathered to earn their daily bread, the Torah was read and interpreted, and the Courts were to be in session.

Listen to the account of this innovation, as we read it in the Book of Nehemiah [8:4ff]:

> And Ezra the Scribe stood upon a pulpit of wood, which they had made for the purpose; and beside them stood Mattithiah and Shema and Anaiah and Uriah and Hilkiah and Maaseiah on his right hand; and on his left hand Pedaiah and Mishael and Malchiah and Hashum and Hashbadana, Zechariah and Meshullam. . . . And the Levites caused the people to understand the law; and the people stood in their place. So they *read in the book of the law distinctly, and gave the sense, and caused them to understand the reading.*

Here, with the reference to those "who read in the book of the law distinctly and gave the sense, and caused them to understand the reading," we have the first clue to the origins of the *darshan.*

Some time thereafter we become aware of the structure of the *meturgeman. Meturgeman* is an Aramaic word that means "one who translates," but the "one who translates" became also the "one who interprets."

The fact that the earliest term for this craft is Aramaic and not Hebrew is very significant. Recall the destruction of the First Temple, and the letter of Jeremiah to the exiles. Recall that the Babylonian community persisted and grew, always out of reach of the Roman expansion. Recall how after the destruction of the Second Commonwealth, it was Rabbinic Judaism of the long-range messianic type that moved first to Jabneh, then to the Galilee, and finally back to the Parthian Empire, out of the reach of Rome.

The Judaism that developed thus developed among Jews whose language was no longer Hebrew. Their language was Aramaic, the lingua franca of the Middle East. By the second century, even the Galilee had become Aramaicized. It was Jews from Babylonia who returned with Ezra and Nehemiah to build the Second Temple. It is doubtful that most of them by this time knew Hebrew well.

The change-over probably began with the Assyrian destruction of the Northern Kingdom, Israel, and the siege of Jerusalem, which as you may recall was miraculously terminated because of a plague in the Assyrian forces. However, at the height of the siege, and a bitter siege it was, reminiscent of the later Roman siege, the Assyrian General Rab Shakeh called for surrender as he parlayed with the leaders.

Here is how it is recorded:

> Then said Eliakim, the son of Hilkiah, and Shebna, and Joah unto Rab Shakeh: "Speak, I pray thee to thy servants in the Aramean language; for we understand it; and speak not with us in the Jews' language, in the ears of the people that are on the wall." . . . [Despite this plea] Rab Shakeh stood and cried with a loud voice in the Jews' language, and spoke, saying. . . . [2K18:26f]

Language process changes do not occur overnight. Within a space of perhaps three centuries from the Assyrian invasion to the years following the confrontation with Babylonia and the destruction of Jerusalem, the change takes place, and Aramaic becomes the language of a majority of the people. And according to tradition, Rav Shakeh who spoke for the Assyrians was a convert from Judaism.

Evidence of this Aramaicization is to be found in the books of Ezra and Nehemiah, as well as in the Book of Daniel, where significant portions are in Aramaic. The Kaddish prayer itself, used at the conclusion of the period of study, and in the Hebrew liturgy to act as a division between the sections of the service, and to serve as a prayer for the dead, was in Aramaic.

So it becomes clear that the public reading of the Torah meant translation into Hebrew by the *meturgeman*. This was his principal role, as it developed in Babylonia. The Torah would first be read in Hebrew, and then translated into Aramaic. These Aramaic translations have persisted, as Targum, and to this day are printed side by side in the Rabbinic texts of the Bible. In fact, the custom persisted, long after Aramaic ceased to be the current language of Jews, to read the weekly portion of the Torah at home once in Hebrew and twice in Aramaic.

Although there are no collections of early sermons of this period, a careful reading of the Targumim illustrates that these were not simply direct translations of the texts. They were expansions and amplification, such as a later preacher or *darshan* would do. It is indeed an early echo of the preaching process.

Let us examine a few passages to see exactly how this took place:

In the second version of the Creation Story, in Genesis 2:7, we read:

> And the Lord formed man of the dust of the ground, and breathed into his nostrils the breath of life; and Adam became a living creature.

The Targum to the last phrase is more than just a translation. It reads: "and it became in Adam the spirit of uttering speech." The *meturgeman* is not simply translating *nefesh haya*, he is exegeting it. He is suggesting that the power of speech was the unique quality of Adam, as, by implication, the power of speech through *derashah* was a unique quality for the Jewish people in the spread of Torah.

Then we come to the story of the Garden of Eden and the expulsion of Adam and Eve because of the temptation of the serpent. Adam is told that because of this sin he would henceforth earn his bread by the sweat of his brow. Eve is informed that she would bear children in pain. And to the serpent God says:

> And I will put enmity between thee and the woman, and between thy seed and her seed; it shall bruise thy head, and thou shalt bruise his heel. [Genesis 3:15]

The Targum to the last phrase is not simply a translation of "it shall bruise thy head, and thou shalt bruise his heel" but an elaboration, which again has the germ of a homily, if not given in full, then at least clearly suggested: "He [mankind] will remind you of what you did to him in the past, and you will preserve your hatred for him into the future." From the beginning the serpent/human relationship had a deep and enduring psychological impact.

When Adam and Eve sinned, God had a twinge of regret for having created them. After all, He had, according to one midrash, been warned against this by a group of His angels, but He had ignored the advice. In any event we read: "And God repented that He had made man on earth and it grieved him at his heart." [Genesis 6:6] The translation to this comes out as: "He determined upon breaking their power according to his will." Quite a change, is it not? Not man's downfall, but his defeat by God through man's loss of power is central. We almost hear an echo of the Prometheus myth!

Another instance deals with the moment at Mount Sinai after the people have heard the Ten Commandments proclaimed, and have cried out with one voice: "All the words which the Lord hath said, we will do." After which Moses, Aaron, Nadab and Abihu go up to the mountain for a revelation of the divine, and the heavens are opened in all their radiant glory for the people to see. The people are included in this experience:

> And upon the nobles of the Children of Israel he laid
> not his hand; also they saw God and they did eat and
> drink. [Exodus 25:11]

This passage troubled the meturgeman. The image of feasting at such a moment, an act of total self-indulgence, was not to his liking. Hence his translation reads:

> They beheld God's glory and gladly offered sacrifices
> which were received with favor *as though they had eaten
> and drunk.*

Furthermore, we find on some occasions that the variants of translation in the Targum are clearly linked to a Talmudic tradition, which had by this time developed. For example, in the legal code that follows the proclamation of the Ten Commandments in Exodus, where the damages for injury are recorded, we read:

If he then gets up and walks outdoors upon his staff,
the assailant shall go unpunished, except that he must
pay for his idleness and for his cure. [Exodus 21:19]

The Targum reads: "he shall pay him for the hire of a physi-
cian," which is exactly the formula we find in the Talmud. Simi-
larly, in Deuteronomy where we are told that the Levites shall
have equal portions to eat except for that which is sold according
to their patrimony [Deuteronomy 18:8], Targum reads: "They
shall have equal portions to eat except for that which accrues to
them from their tour of duty, for thus their fathers have decreed." What is vague in the Torah text comes out clearly as their
daily wage, and it is thus specified in the Talmud. [Sukkah 56a].

Here then are glimpses of how the *meturgeman* functioned,
and what he did by way of not only interpreting but expounding
the Torah. We have to dig for the evidence, and ferret it out, but
when it is put together, the portrait begins to emerge.

We watch this role of *meturgeman* grow and expand, as the
process of Rabbinic exegesis develops and the Talmud emerges.
There was a two level process of communication. The sage
taught his students in smaller groups, but as these grew in size,
and the sages were not always good speakers, they required
someone who could do this for them.

Such a role was known as *meturgeman* or *amora*. The commentator Rashi, who in the eleventh century in the Rhineland wrote
the classic commentary of the Talmud, making its study possible
in the West, found it necessary to describe the role as follows:

Amora—the translator who stands at the side of the
preaching sage while the latter quietly whispers to him
in Hebrew what he wishes to say, while the former translates it into the language the people understand. [Rashi
to Yoma 20b and Ketubot 106a]

In another source [Ket. 106a] we learn that Rav Huna had thirteen *meturgemanim*, so large were his classes. They were scattered
throughout the audience and "they listened to what he said and
repeated it to the assembly on either side, and from the front

and rear of the audience, positioning themselves in every section of the crowd." [Ketubot 106a]

In the preceding chapter, we indicated that one of the causes suggested for Elisha ben Abuya's lapse into heresy was that he saw the martyrdom of the greatest preacher of his time, Huzpit the *Meturgeman*, whose tongue he saw devoured by dogs. That such eloquence could come to such an end was more than he could bear.

It was said of Huzpit that he studied the book of Leviticus 170 times and was compared in brilliance to Jonathan ben Uzziel, who was one of Johanan ben Zakkai's most brilliant disciples. When he spoke, "his mouth uttered pearls."

How would a lecture be stopped? If it was deemed improper it was stopped with the command: "Remove the *meturgeman*." In our own time they would say: "Turn off the public address system!" For example, it was related that one time when Rabban Gamliel was publicly insulting Rabbi Joshua ben Hananiah, the Sages put an end to it by ordering Huzpit the *Meturgeman* to halt!

We find here and there in the Talmud the listing by name of the meturgeman to a given scholar. Judah the Prince, the man who finally edited the Mishnah [circa 200], had a *meturgeman* whose name was Abba Yudan [Jerusalem Talmud, Berakhot 1:1]. Rav, his son-in-law, who with Samuel moved the academies to Babylonia, was the meturgeman for his uncle Hiyya and for the great sage Shila. [Yoma 20b] We are informed that he had a special talent as a popular *darshan*, that he had a very attractive voice, and often acted as cantor. [Teshuvat ha Geonim, Sha'arei Teshuva 178] Judah ben Nahmani was *meturgeman* for Simeon ben Lakish [Hagiga 15a], Bar Yehuda was *meturgeman* for Abbahu [Megillah 14:7] and Rabbi Pedat was *meturgeman* for Yissa.

The mere citation of these names and references shows the wide prevalence of the *darshan/meturgeman* role.

One need only look into the Code of Maimonides, in which the whole corpus of Talmudic exegesis and development is fixed and codified as Judaism develops in the middle ages to the modern era, to see how this role emerges as a fixed institution in the process of teaching and continuing Judaism.

In the section dealing with the laws surrounding the study

of Torah, the entire gamut of this process that is at the heart of Judaism is explored in direct and pithy statements as to what is required.

Dealing with how a teacher must teach, how the teacher must relate to his students, and the students to their master, does one sit or does one stand when a class is in session, does the teacher stand and the class sit, or vice versa, who respects whom and how, what are the grounds for excommunicating a teacher and a student, when must a busy person study, we suddenly encounter the following:

> If he [the Sage] was teaching through a *meturgeman*, the [*meturgeman*] between him and his students, the Sage speaks to the *meturgeman* and the *meturgeman* speaks to all the students. When they [the students] ask a question of the *meturgeman*, he asks the Sage and the Sage gives the answer to the *meturgeman*, and the *meturgeman* gives the answer to the students. . . .

If you think this is a strange process, let me hasten to assure you that it isn't. I cannot help, at this juncture, but recall my visit to Cracow in 1982. My book on David Darshan of Cracow was about to appear, and that year, the Dean of the Pontifical Academy of Theology in Cracow, who had been visiting the Catholic Theological Union in Chicago, had heard of this. When he heard that I would be teaching in Jerusalem that fall, he thought it would be a good idea if I would stop in Cracow to lecture about David Darshan in his home town!

I thought it would be a good idea too—in fact, a great idea. The only problem was that I couldn't speak Polish and the students knew no English. For my host it was no problem. He offered to act as *meturgeman*, though he didn't know the term. And he was so good and so swift in his translation that immediate rapport with the students was achieved. They even laughed at my bad jokes!

I would speak a few sentences, and he would translate them. And the questions—there were many, intense, probing, from students, some of whom were Solidarity activists who had just been freed from prison; they were asked in Polish, translated to English, answered in English and translated back into Polish. Take my word for it, it worked, and I can assure you that it worked as well, if not better, in the process developed by Ezra and continued through the generations.

What Maimonides was here describing was clearly something institutionalized and part of the learning process. What is more, there was a whole series of mutual obligations and a whole ethic of relationship. See how he continues:

> The Sage may not speak louder than the *meturgeman*, nor shall the *meturgeman* speak louder than the Sage when he asks a question of the Sage. The *meturgeman* may neither subtract from nor add to what the Sage has said, nor may he change anything unless he happens to be the Sage's father or teacher. . . .

What we see is a carefully balanced and orchestrated relationship designed to respect the status of each. One perceptive commentator raised the question, and rightly so, that if the class were large, the *meturgeman* would have to speak louder than he spoke to the Sage. And the answer comes through in the affirmative. But the mutual respect is what is really important.

The commentator invokes God to make his point, and God, in this connection, is given the role of *meturgeman!* Remember how at the beginning of the lecture I suggested that God was the first preacher?

How does the commentator make the deduction? By describing the moment at Sinai when God and Moses spoke to each other. He quotes the account from Exodus: "And the voice of the horn waxed louder and louder, Moses spoke and God answered him by a voice." The question is: With what kind of voice? Being God's, was it louder and more powerful, as clearly it had to be? No, came the answer. God responded to Moses in exactly the same level of voice with which Moses spoke, just as any good *meturgeman* was required to do! [Numbers Rabbah XIV: 3]

The road from exegete to preacher, from *midrash* to *Dar-*

shan, has been traversed in this volume. Rabbinic Judaism and early Christianity came out of the same source, developed in the creative years of the Second Commonwealth. They emerged as reactions to the cataclysmic end of that commonwealth. They shared and developed a common basis in sacred text, spread its word, each according to its own light, through the spoken word.

Rabbinic Texts

Most of the texts in the supplement are derived from the Soncino Translations of the Babylonian Talmud and of the Midrash Rabbah. Passages from the Jerusalem Talmud are identified with the letter J. preceding the name of the tractate. References with an * were translated by the author.

SUPPLEMENT: CHAPTER THREE

Rabbinic Texts: Simeon ben Shetah

- 1 -

King Jannai and his queen were taking a meal together. Now after he had put the Rabbis to death, there was no one to say grace for them. He said to his spouse: "I wish we had someone to say grace for us." She said to him: "Swear to me that if I bring you one you will not harm him." He swore to her, and she brought him Simeon ben Shetah, her brother. She placed him between her husband and herself, saying: "See what honor I pay you." He replied: "It is not you who honor me but it is the Torah which honors me." He [Jannai] said to her: "You see that he does not acknowledge any authority!" They gave him a cup of wine to say grace over. He said: "How shall I say grace? [Shall I say] 'Blessed is He of whose sustenance Jannai and his companions have eaten?'" So he drank that cup, and they gave him another, and he said grace over it . . .

-BERAKHOT 48A

- 2 -

What is the reason for *Hanukkah*? For our Rabbis taught: On the twenty-fifth of Kislev the days of *Hanukkah*, which are eight commence on which a lamentation for the dead and fasting are forbidden. For when the Greeks entered the Temple, they defiled all the oils therein, and when the Hasmonean dynasty prevailed against them and defeated them, they searched and found only one cruse of oil which lay with the seal of the High Priest, but which contained sufficient for one day's lighting only. Yet a miracle occurred and they lit [the lamp] with that oil for eight days. The following year these [days] were appointed a Festival with [the recital of] Hallel and thanksgiving.

-SHABBAT 21B

- *3* -

What was the incident with Rabbi Joshua ben Perahia? When King Jannai put the Rabbis to death, Simeon ben Shetah was hid by his sister, whilst Rabbi Joshua ben Perahia fled to Alexandria in Egypt. When there was peace, Simeon ben Shetah sent [this message to him]: "From me, Jerusalem, the holy city, to you Alexandria in Egypt. O my sister, my husband dwells in your midst and I abide desolate." [Rabbi Joshua] arose and came back and found himself in a certain inn where they paid him great respect. He said: "How beautiful is this *aksania!*" One of his disciples [Jesus of Nazareth] said to him: "My master, her eyes are narrow!" He replied to him: "Wicked person! Is it with such thoughts that you occupy yourself?" He sent forth four hundred horns and excommunicated him. [The disciple] came before him on many occasions, saying: "Receive me!" but he refused to notice him. One day while Rabbi Joshua was reciting the *shema,* he came before him. His intention was to receive him and he made a sign to him with his hand, but the disciple thought that he was repelling him. So he went and set up a brick* and worshipped it. Rabbi Joshua said to him: "Repent!" But he answered him: "Thus have I received from you that whoever sinned and caused others to sin is deprived of the power of doing penitence." A master has said: "The disciple practiced magic and led Israel astray."

-SOTAH 47A

*A suggested emendation of the text that reads *levinta* [brick] to read *tselavta* [cross] is plausible. This interpretation was used by Rabbi Yehiel of Paris in a disputation with Christians in 1240.

- 4 -

Rabbi Jeremiah asked: "Can grace be recited in common by including one who has dined on vegetables?" [The question may be answered by the following incident]. Three hundred nazirites came up in the days of Simeon ben Shetah. He found grounds for absolution for one hundred and fifty, but for the other hundred and fifty he could find no grounds. Accordingly he repaired to King Jannai and said to him: "Three hundred nazirites have come up and need nine hundred sacrifices. You give half and I will give half." Jannai did so, but a talebearer went and informed him that Simeon had given nothing. When Simeon learned this he fled. Some time after, certain Persian dignitaries were dining at King Jannai's table, and they observed: "We remember that there used to be an old man here who spoke to us words of wisdom." He said to his sister: "Send for him to come here." "Give him your promise of safety," she retorted, "and he will come." The promise having been given, he came and sat between the king and the queen. "What is the meaning of this?" he [Jannai] demanded. "[I do this] because it is written in the Book of Ben Sirah: 'Esteem her [sc. knowledge] and she shall exalt you and seat you between princes,'" he replied. "Why did you fool me?" he asked. "Heaven forfend! I did not fool you, but you gave of yours, while I gave of mine [i.e. knowledge]" . . .

-GENESIS RABBA XCI.3

- 5 -

THE KING MAY NEITHER JUDGE, etc. Rabbi Joseph said: This refers only to the kings of Israel, but the kings of the House of David may judge and be judged. . . . But why this prohibition of the kings of Israel? Because of an incident which happened with a slave of King Jannai who killed a man. Simeon ben Shetah said to the Sages: "Set your eyes boldly upon him and let us judge him." So they sent the King word saying: "Your slave has killed a man." Thereupon he sent him to them to be tried. But they again sent him a message: "You too must come here, for the Torah says 'If warning has been given to its owners,' [teaching] that the owner of the ox must come and stand by his ox." The King accordingly came and sat down. Then Simeon ben Shetah said: "Stand on your feet, King Jannai, and let the witnesses testify against thee; yet it is not before us that you stand, but before Him who spoke and the world came into being . . ." "I shall not act in accordance with what you say, but in accordance with what your colleagues say," he answered. Simeon then turned first to the right, and then to the left, but they all for fear of the king looked down at the ground. Then said Simeon ben Shetah unto them: "Are you wrapped in thoughts? Let the Master of thoughts [God] come and call you to account." Instantly, Gabriel came and smote them to the ground, and they died. It was there and then enacted: A King [not of the House of David] may neither judge nor be judged, testify nor be testified against.

-SANHEDRIN 19A

- 6 -

It is related of Rabbi Simeon ben Shetah that he once bought an ass from an Ishmaelite [i.e. an Arab]. His disciples came and found a precious stone suspended from its neck. They said to him: "Master, 'The blessing of the Lord enriches' [Proverbs 10:22]." Rabbi Simeon ben Shetah replied: "I have purchased an ass, but I have not purchased a precious stone." He then went and returned it to the Ishmaelite and the latter exclaimed of him: "Blessed be the Lord God of Simeon ben Shetah." Thus from the faithfulness of man we learn the faithfulness of God, who is faithful to pay the reward of the precepts which Israel perform.

-DEUTERONOMY RABBAH iii:3

- 7 -

It was taught: Jose ben Joezer of Zeredah and Jose ben Johanan of Jerusalem decreed uncleanness in respect of the country of the heathens and glassware. Simeon ben Shetah instituted the woman's marriage settlement and imposed uncleanness upon metal utensils. Shammai and Hillel decreed uncleanness for the hands.

-SHABBAT 14B

- 8 -

Rab Judah stated: At first they used to give merely a written undertaking in respect of the *ketubah* of a virgin for two hundred zuz, and in respect of that of a widow for a *maneh* [i.e. one hundred *zuz*], and consequently they grew old and could not take any wives, when Simeon ben Shetah took the initiative and ordained that all the property of a husband is pledged for the *ketubah* of his wife.

-KETUBOTH 82B

- 9 -

It has been taught: Rabbi Simeon ben Shetah said: May I never see comfort if I did not see a man pursuing a fellow into a ruin, and when I ran after him and saw him, sword in hand with blood dripping from it, and the murdered man writhing, I exclaimed to him: "Wicked man, who slew this man? It is either you or I! But what can I do, since your life does not rest in my hands, for it is written in the Torah, 'At the mouth of two witnesses . . . shall he that is to die be put to death?' [Deuteronomy 17:6]. May he who knows one's thoughts exact vengeance from him who slew his fellow! It is related that before they moved from the place a serpent came and bit the murderer so that he died."

-SANHEDRIN 37B

- 10 -

What is the case of one behaving familiarly with heaven? As we have learnt: Simeon ben Shetah sent to Honi the Circle-maker and said: "You deserve to be excommunicated, and were you not Honi, I would pronounce excommunication against you. But what can I do seeing that you ingratiate yourself with the Omnipresent and He performs your desires, and you are like the son who ingratiates himself with his father and he performs his desires?"

-BERAKHOT 19A

- 11 -

Abaye also said: Whence do I know it? Because it was taught: It once happened that King Jannai went to Kohalith in the wilderness and conquered sixty towns there. On his return he rejoiced exceedingly and invited all the sages of Israel. Said he to them: "Our forefathers ate mallows when they were engaged in the building of the [Second] Temple; let us eat mallows in memory of our forefathers." So mallows were served on golden tables and they ate. Now there was a man there, frivolous, evil-hearted and worthless, named Eleazar son of Poirah, who said to King Jannai: "O King Jannai, the hearts of the Pharisees are against you." "Then what shall I do?" "Test them by the plate between your eyes." Now an elder named Gedidiah was present there. Said he to King Jannai: "O King Jannai! Let the royal crown suffice for you, and leave the priestly crown to the seed of Aaron." [For it was rumored that his mother had been taken captive in Modi'im.] Accordingly, the charge was investigated but not sustained, and the Sages of Israel departed in anger. Then said Eliezer ben Poirah to King Jannai: "O King Jannai! That is the law for the most humble man in Israel, and you, a King and a High Priest, shall that be your law too?" "Then what shall I do?" "If you will take my advice, trample them down." "But what shall happen with the Torah?" "Behold, it is rolled up and lying in the corner. Whoever wishes to study let him go and study." Said Rabbi Nahman ben Isaac: "Immediately a spirit of heresy was instilled into him, for he should have replied, 'That is well for the Written Law; but what of the Oral Law?' " Immediately the evil burst forth through Eleazar ben Poirah, all the sages of Israel were massacred and the world was desolate until Simeon ben Shetah came and restored the Torah to its pristine glory.

-KIDDUSHIN, 66A

- 12 -

Our Rabbis have taught. There are seven types of Pharisees: the *shikmi* Pharisee, the *kizai* Pharisee, the "pestle" Pharisee [who constantly exclaims] "What is my duty that I may perform it?", the Pharisee from love of God and the Pharisee from fear. The *shikmi* Pharisee—he is one who performs the action of Shechem [who was circumcised from an unworthy metive]. The *nikpi* Pharisee—he is one who knocks his feet together [i.e. walks with exaggerated humility]. The *kizai* Pharisee—Rabbi Nahman ben Isaac said: "He is one who makes his blood flow against the walls [i.e. a calculating Pharisee, who performs a good deed and then a bad deed]. The "pestle" Pharisee—Rabbi ben Shila said: "[His head] is bowed like [a pestle in] a mortar." The Pharisee who constantly exclaims: "What is my duty that I may perform it?"— but that is a virtue—Nay, what he says is: "What further duty is there that I may perform it?" The Pharisee from love and the Pharisee from fear. . . . King Jannai said to his wife: "Fear not the Pharisees and the non-Pharisees but the hypocrites who ape the Pharisees; because their deeds are the deeds of Zimri, but they expect a reward like Phineas."

-SOTAH 22A

SUPPLEMENT: CHAPTER FOUR

Rabbinic Texts: Hillel

- 1 -

What does "He would utterly be condemned" mean? Ulla said: Not like Simeon the brother of Azariah nor like Rabbi Johanan of the Prince's house but like Hillel and Shebna. Once Rabbi Dimi came and related that Hillel and Shebna were brothers. Hillel engaged in [the study of] Torah and Shebna was occupied in business. One day [Shebna] said to him, "Come, let us become partners and divide [the profits]." A *Bath Kol* issued for and proclaimed . . . "No!"

-SOTAH 21A

- 2 -

Our Sages taught: The poor, the rich, the sensual come before the heavenly court. They say to the poor: "Why did you not occupy yourself with Torah?" If he says: "I was poor and worried about my livelihood," they would say to him: "Were you poorer than Hillel?" It was reported about Hillel the Elder that every day he used to work and earn one *tropoaik*, of which he would give half to the guard at the House of Study, and use the other half for his food and for that of his family. One day he found nothing to earn and the guard of the House of Study would not permit him to enter. He climbed up to the roof and sat over the skylight, to hear the words of the living God from the mouth of

141

Shemaiah and Abtalyon. They say that it was the eve of the Sabbath in mid-winter and snow fell down upon him from heaven. When the dawn rose, Shemaiah said to Abtalyon: "Brother Abtalion, on every day this house is light and today it is dark. Could it perhaps be a cloudy day?" They looked up and saw the figure of a man in the window. They went up and found him covered with three cubits of snow. They removed him, bathed him, placed him opposite the fire and said: "This man deserves that the Sabbath be profaned on his behalf!"

-YOMA 35B

- 3 -

Forty years before the Temple was destroyed the Sanhedrin went into exile and took its seat in the Trade Halls. To what law does this refer? Said Rabbi Isaac ben Abdimi: "To teach that they did not hand down decisions in laws of fines." That was not the case. Rather "They did not hand down decisions in capital cases." And should you answer that they [Jose ben Joezer and Jose ben Johanan] flourished during these eighty years too, surely it was taught: Hillel and Simeon [his son], Gamliel and Simeon were Patriarchs during one hundred years of the Temple's existence, while Jose ben Joezer of Zereda and Jose ben Johanan were much earlier!

-SHABBAT 15A

- 4 -

Hillel the Elder expounded seven exegetical laws in the presence of the Sons of Bathyra, viz. the inference drawn from a minor premise to a major; the inference drawn from a similarity of words and phrases; a general principle established on the basis of a law contained in one verse or of laws contained in two verses; the rule when a generalization is followed in the text by a specification, and when a specification is found in the text by a generalization; the inference drawn from an analogous passage elsewhere; the interpretation of a word or passage from its context. These are the seven rules which Hillel the Elder expounded in the presence of the Sons of Bathyra.

-ABOTH D'RABBI NATHAN 32A

- 5 -

Hillel the Elder was wont to interpret ordinary speech. For it has been taught: When the Alexandrians used to betroth their wives, and were about to take them for the *huppah* ceremony, strangers would come and abduct them. Thereupon the Sages wished to declare their children bastards. Hillel the Elder said to them: Bring me your mother's *ketubahs*. When they brought them, he found written therein: "When you are taken for the *huppah*, be my wife." And on the strength of this they did not declare their children bastards.

-BABA MEZIA 104A

- 6 -

Our Sages taught: This *halakhah* was forgotten by the Sons of Bathyra. On one occasion the fourteenth [of Nisan] fell on the Sabbath and they forgot the ruling whether the Passover overrides the Sabbath or not. Said they: "Is there anyone who knows whether the Passover overrides the Sabbath or not?" They told: "There is a certain person who has come up from Babylonia, Hillel the Babylonian by name, who served the two greatest men of the time, and he knows whether the Passover overrides the

Sabbath or not." So they summoned him and said to him: "Do you know whether the Passover overrides the Sabbath or not?" "Do we only have one Passover during the year which overrides the Sabbath?" was his reply. "Surely we have many more than two hundred Passovers during the year which override the Sabbath!" They said to him: "How do you know it?" He answered them: "*In its appointed time* is stated in connection with the Passover, and *In its appointed time* is stated in connection with the *tamid*. Just as *Its appointed time* which is said in connection with the *tamid* overrides the Sabbath, so *Its appointed time* which is said in connection with the Passover overrides the Sabbath. Moreover, it follows *a minori:* if the omission of the *tamid* which is not punished by *kareth* [death], overrides the Sabbath, then Passover is punished by *kareth* if it is not done, it is logical that it should override the Sabbath!" They immediately set him at their head and appointed him Patriarch over them. Thereafter he sat and instructed them on the laws of Passover. He began rebuking them. He said to them: "Why was it necessary for me to come up from Babylonia to be a Patriarch over you? It was your laziness, because you did not serve the two greatest men of the time, Shemaiah and Abtalyon." They said to him: "Master, what if the person forgot and did not bring a knife on the eve of the Sabbath?" "I once knew this law" he replied, "but have forgotten it. But leave it to Israel, for if they are not prophets, they are sons of prophets!" The next day, if the Passover offering was a lamb, the knife was placed in its wool, and if it was a goat it was placed between its horns. He saw the incident and recollected the *halakhah* and said: "Indeed, that is the tradition I received directly from Shemaiah and Abtalyon."

-PESAHIM 66A

- 7 -

Our Sages taught: One should always be gentle like Hillel and not impatient like Shammai. One time it happened that two men made a wager saying, "Whichever of us can make Hillel lose his temper will receive four hundred zuz." Said one: "I will go and try." That day was eve of Sabbath, and Hillel was washing his head. He went, passed by the door of his house, and called out: "Is Hillel here? Is Hillel here?" So Hillel dressed and went out to him, saying: "My son, what do you require?" "I have a question to ask," said he. "Ask, my son," he countered. Thereupon he asked: "Why are the heads of the Babylonians round?" "My son, you have asked a great question," replied he, "because they have skillful midwives." He departed, waited a while, returned, and called out: "Is Hillel here? Is Hillel here?" He dressed and went out to him saying, "My son, what do you require?" "I have a question to ask," said he. "Ask, my son," he replied. Thereupon he asked: "Why are the eyes of the Palmyrians bleary?" "My son, you have asked a great question," replied he, "because they live in sandy places." He left, waited a while, and called out: "Is Hillel here? Is Hillel here?" He dressed and went out to him saying: "My son, what do you require?" "I have a question to ask," said he. "Ask, my son," he replied. He asked: "Why are the feet of the Africans wide?" "My son, you have asked a great question," said he, "because they live in watery marshes." "I have many questions to ask," said he, "but fear that you may become angry." Thereupon he sat before him and said: "Ask all the questions you have to ask." "Are you the Hillel who is called the Patriarch of all Israel?" "Yes," he replied. "If that is you," he retorted, "may there not be many like you in Israel." "Why, my son?" he asked. "Because I have lost four hundred zuz because of you," he growled. "Be careful of your moods," he answered, "as far as Hillel is concerned, it is better that you lose four hundred *zuz* and still four hundred more, and Hillel not lose his temper."

Our Sages taught: A certain gentile once came before Shammai and asked him: "How many Torahs have you?" "Two," he replied, "the Written Torah and the Oral Torah." "I can accept your teaching with respect to the Written Torah, but not the Oral Torah. Convert me to Judaism on condition that you teach me the Written Torah only." But he scolded him and drove him away in anger. When he went before Hillel, he accepted him as a proselyte. On the first day he taught him, *alef, bet, gimel, daleth;* the following day he reversed them to him. "But yesterday did you not teach them to me thus?" he protested. "Must you then not rely upon me? Then rely upon me with respect to the Oral Torah." On another occasion it happened that a certain gentile came before Shammai and said to him: "You may convert me on condition that you teach me the whole Torah while I stand on one foot." Thereupon he repulsed him with the builder's cubit which was in his hand. When he went before Hillel he said to him: "What is hateful to you, do not to your neighbor. That is the whole Torah, the rest is commentary. Go and study it."

On another occasion it happened that a certain gentile was passing behind a school house when he heard the voice of a teacher reciting: *And these are the garments which they shall make: a breastplate and an ephod.* [Exodus 28:4] Said he, "For whom are these?" "For the High Priest," he was told. Then said the heathen to himself, "I will go and become a convert, that I may be appointed a High Priest." So he went before Shammai and said to him: "Convert me on condition you make me a High Priest." But he drove him away with the builder's cubit that was in his hand. Then he went before Hillel, who converted him. Said he to him: "Can any man be made king but he who knows the arts of government? Go and study the arts of government!" He went and studied, and when he came to: *"and the stranger that comes near shall be put to death"* he asked him: "To whom does this verse apply?" "Even to King David of Israel." The convert therefore reasoned using the *a fortiori* argument: "If Israel, who are called the sons of the Eternal and whom, in His love for them he designated his sons, and yet it is written of them *and the stranger that comes near is to be put to death*; how much more so an ordinary convert who comes with his staff and his wallet!" Then he went before Shammai and said to him: "Am I then eligible to be a High Priest? Is it not written in the Torah: *and the stranger that comes near shall be put to death?*" He went before Hillel and said to him: "O gentle Hillel, a blessing on you for bringing me under the wings of the *Shekhinah!*" Some time later, the three of them met in one place. Said they:

Shammai's impatience sought to drive us from the world, but Hillel's goodness brought us under the wings of the *Shekhinah*.

-SHABBAT 30B

- 8 -

Rabbi Abba said in the name of Samuel: "There was a dispute between the House of Shammai and the House of Hillel that lasted three years. The former asserted: 'The *halakhah* is in agreement with our views', and the latter arguing: 'The *halakhah* is in agreement with our views.' Then a Voice from Heaven announced: Both are the words of the Living God; however the *halakha* is in agreement with the rulings of the House of Hillel." Since, however, "both are the words of the Living God" what was it that entitled the House of Hillel to have the *halakhah* fixed in agreement with them? Because they were kindly and modest. They studied their own rulings and those of the House of Shammai, and were even so humble as to mention the actions of the House of Shammai before theirs. . . .

Our Sages taught: The House of Shammai and the House of Hillel debated for two and a half years whether it were better for a human being to have been created or not, the House of Shammai taking the former position, and the House of Hillel arguing the latter. They finally voted and agreed that it were better for man not to have been created, but now that he has been created, let him investigate his past deeds, or, as others say, let him examine his future actions.

-ERUVIN 13B

- *9* -

One day, after the study period was ended, Hillel walked along with his disciples. They asked him, "Master, where are you going?" He replied, "To perform a religious duty." "Can you tell us what that religious duty is?" they asked. "To take a bath," he replied. "That's a religious duty?" they asked, incredulously. "Yes, indeed," he replied, "for if the statues of kings, which are erected in theatres and circuses are scoured and washed by the man appointed to look after them. . . . how much more I who have been created in the Image and the Likeness!" [Gen. 9:6]

SUPPLEMENT: CHAPTER FIVE

Rabbinic Texts: Johanan ben Zakkai

- 1 -

Hillel the Elder had eighty disciples: thirty of them were worthy that the Divine Presence should rest upon them as upon Moses our teacher, but their generation was not worthy of it; thirty of them were worthy that the intercallation of the years should be determined by them; and twenty were average. The greatest of them all was Jonathan ben Uzziel, and the least of them all was Johanan ben Zakkai. It was said of Rabban Johanan ben Zakkai that he mastered Scripture, Mishnah, *Gemara, halakhot, aggadot, toseftot,* the minutiae of the Torah, the minutiae of the Scribes, and all the hermeneutical rule of the Sages. Not a word in the Torah did he not master . . .

-AVOT D'RABBI NATHAN 24A

- 2 -

Our Rabbis have taught: Hillel the Elder had eighty disciples, thirty of whom were worthy of the Divine Spirit resting upon them, as it did upon Moses our master, thirty of whom were worthy that the sun should stand still for them as it did for Joshua the son of Nun, and the remaining twenty were ordinary. The greatest of them was Jonathan ben Uzziel, the smallest of them was Johanan ben Zakkai. They said of Rabbi Johanan ben Zakkai that he did not leave unstudied Scripture, *Mishnah,*

Gemara, Halakhah, Aggada, details of the Scribes, inferences *a minori ad majus,* analogies, calendrical computations, *gematrias,* the speech of Ministering Angels, the speech of spirits, and the speech of palm trees, fullers parables and fox fables, great matters and small matters. Great matters mean *ma'aseh merkavah,* small matters, the discussions of Abaya and Raba. . . . And if the smallest of them was so great, how much more so was the greatest? They said of Johanan ben Uzziel when he used to sit and occupy himself with the study of the Torah, every bird that flew above him was immediately burnt.

-SUKKAH 28
-BAVA BATRA 134A

- 3 -

When the son of Rabban Johanan ben Zakkai died, his disciples came in to console him. Rabbi Eliezer came and sat before him and said: "My master, is it your wish that I say a word in your presence?" He replied to him: "Speak." Thereupon he said: "Adam, the first man, had a son who died, and he allowed himself to be comforted in his loss . . . therefore do you accept condolence." He retorted: "Is it not sufficient to bear my own grief that you have to mention Adam's grief?" Then Rabbi Joshua entered and said: "My master, is it your wish that I say a word in your presence?" He replied to him: "Speak." Thereupon he said: "Job had sons and daughters who all died in one day and he allowed himself to be comforted; you too accept condolence . . ." He retorted: "Is it not sufficient for me to bear my own grief that you have to mention Job's grief?" Then Rabbi Simeon entered and said: "My master, is it your wish that I say a word in your presence?" He replied: "Speak." Thereupon he said: "King David had a son who died and he allowed himself to be comforted, do you also accept condolence.". . . . He retorted: "Is it not sufficient for me to bear my own grief that you have to mention David's grief?" Finally Rabbi El'azer ben Arak entered . . . and came in and sat before him and said: "Let me tell you a parable. To what is the matter like? To a man with whom a king had deposited an article of value. Daily the man wept and exclaimed: 'Woe is me! When will I be free from the responsibility of this trust?' You too, my master had a son versed in the Torah. . . . He has departed sinless from this world. Surely you should derive comfort from having returned your trust intact!" Rabban Johanan said to him: "El'azer my son, you have comforted me as men can comfort."

When they left his presence, Rabbi El'azer said to his colleagues: "I will go to Dimsith, a delectable place with excellent and refreshing waters." The others said: "We will go to Yavneh, a place abounding with scholars and lovers of Torah." Because he went to Dimsith, a delectable spot with excellent and refreshing waters, his fame in the Torah waned; whereas they who went to Yavneh, a place abounding with scholars and lovers of Torah, their renown in Torah increased.

-AVOT D'RABBI NATHAN 24A

- 4 -

It happened once that Rabbi Johanan ben Zakkai was coming out of Jerusalem, followed by Rabbi Joshua, and he beheld the Temple in ruins. "Woe to us," cried Rabbi Joshua, "for this house that lies in ruins, the place where atonement was made for the sins of Israel!" Rabban Johanan said to him: "My son, be not grieved, for we have another means of atonement which is as effective, and that is the practice of lovingkindness, as it is stated: *For I desire lovingkindness and not sacrifice.*" [Hosea 6:6] And so we find it with Daniel, the man greatly beloved, who devoted himself to acts of lovingkindness. What were the acts of lovingkindness to which Daniel devoted himself? . . . He provided for the bride and made her to rejoice, he attended the dead to the grave, he gave alms to the poor, and prayed three times daily,

and his prayer was accepted with favor, as it is stated: *And when
Daniel knew that the writing was signed, he went into his house—now his
windows were open in his upper chamber toward Jerusalem—and he
kneeled upon his knees three times a day, and prayed, and gave thanks
before his God, as he did aforetime.* [Daniel 6:2]

-AVOT D'RABBI NATHAN 20A

- 5 -

When Vespasian came to destroy Jerusalem, he proclaimed to its
inhabitants: "Fools, why do you seek to destroy this city and burn
the Temple? What do I demand of you? Merely that you deliver
to me one bow or one arrow, and then I will depart from you."
They answered him: "As we went forth against your two predecessors and slew them, so we will go out against you and slay
you." When Rabban Johanan ben Zakkai heard this, he sent for
the men of Jerusalem and said to them: "My sons, why would
you destroy this city and burn the Temple? What does he demand of you? Merely one bow or one arrow, and then he will
depart from you." They answered him: "As we went forth
against his two predecessors and slew them, so will we go out
against him and slay him." Now Vespasian had some men of his
resident within and close to the walls of Jerusalem, and whatever
they heard they wrote upon an arrow which they shot beyond
the wall. [In this manner] they reported that Rabban Johanan
ben Zakkai was among Caesar's friends. So Rabban Johanan ben
Zakkai appealed to the men of Jerusalem. After he had pleaded
with them for several days and they would not agree with him,
he sent for his disciples, Rabbi Eliezer and Rabbi Joshua, and
said to them: "My sons, arise and carry me forth from here.
Make a coffin for me and I will lie in it." [They did so] and Rabbi
Eliezer took hold of it at the head and Rabbi Joshua at the foot,
and they carried him until sunset when they arrived at the gates
of Jerusalem. The gatekeepers asked: "What is this?" They replied: "A dead man. Do you not know that a corpse may not be

kept overnight in Jerusalem?" They said: "If it is a corpse, carry it out." They carried it out, arrived before Vespasian and opened the coffin and Rabban Johanan stood before him. He asked: "You are Rabban Johanan ben Zakkai? Ask what I shall give you." He replied: "I ask for nothing but Yavneh whither I might go and teach my disciples, where I can institute prayers, and observe all the commandments prescribed in the Torah." He said to him: "Go and do all that you wish to perform." Rabban Johanan then said: "May I be permitted to say a word to you?" "Speak," he said. Rabban Johanan then said, "You are about to become Emperor." "How do you know this?" he asked, and Rabban Johanan replied: "There is a tradition with us that the Temple will not be delivered into the hand of a common soldier, but to a king". . . . It is related that a few days had not elapsed before there came to him a dispatch from Rome, informing him that Caesar had died, and he had been elected Emperor.

They brought to him a battering ram which he directed towards the wall of Jerusalem. Then they brought to him logs of cedar which he inserted in the battering ram and hurled at the wall until he breached it. They then brought to him a pig's head which he inserted in the battering ram and shot it on to the sacrficial limbs that were on the altar. At that moment Jerusalem was captured. Rabban Johanan was sitting and anxiously waiting for news, as Eli had sat and waited for news, as it is stated: *Lo, Eli sat upon his seat by the wayside, watching, for his heart trembled for the ark of God.* [1 Samuel 4:13] As soon as Rabban Johanan ben Zakkai heard that Jerusalem was destroyed and the Temple in flames, he rent his clothes, his disciples also rent their clothes, and they wept and cried aloud and mourned . . .

—AVOT D'RABBI NATHAN 20A

- 6 -

The *biryoni* were then in the city. The Rabbis said to them: "Let us go out and make peace with them [the Romans]." They would not let them, but on the contrary said: "Let us go out and fight them." The Rabbis said: "you will not succeed." They [the *biryoni*] rose up and burnt the stores of wheat and barley so that a famine ensued. . . .

Abba Sikra the head of the *biryoni* in Jerusalem was the son of the sister of Rabban Johanan ben Zakkai. [The latter] said to him, saying: "Come to visit me privately." When he came, he said to him: "How long are you going to carry on this way and kill all the people with starvation?" He replied: "What can I do? If I say a word to them they will kill me." He said: "Devise some plan for me to escape. Perhaps I shall be able to save a little." He said to him: "Pretend to be ill, and let everyone come and inquire about you. Bring something evil smelling and put it by you so that they will say you are dead. Let your disciples get under your bed, but no others, so that they shall not notice that you are still light, since they know that a living being is lighter than a corpse." He did so, and Rabbi Eliezer went under the bier from one side and Rabbi Joshua from the other. When they reached the door some men wanted to put a lance through the bier. He said to them: "Shall the Romans say: They have pierced their master?" They wanted to give it a push. He said to them: "Shall they say they pushed their master?" They opened a town gate for him, and he got out.

When he reached the Romans, he said: "Peace to you, O king, peace to you, O king." Vespasian said: "Your life is forfeit on two counts, one, because I am not a king and you call me a king; and again, if I am a king why did you not come to me before now." He replied: "As for your saying you are not a king, in truth you are a king, since if you were not a king, Jerusalem would not be delivered into your hand, as it is written: *And Lebanon shall fall by a mighty one.* [Isaiah 10;34] *Mighty one* is a term applied only to a king [cf. Jeremiah 30:21] . . . As for your question, why, if you are a king, I did not come till now, the answer if that the *biryoni* among us did not let me." He said to him: "If there is a jar of honey round which a serpent is wound, would they not break the jar to get rid of the serpent?" He could give no answer. "Rabbi Joseph, or some say Rabbi Akiva applied to him the verse, *God turns wise men backwards and makes their knowledge foolish.* [Isaiah 44:25] He ought to have said to him: "We take a pair of tongs and grip the snake and kill it, and leave the jar intact."

At this point a messenger came to him from Rome saying: "Up, for the Emperor is dead and the notables of Rome have decided to make you head [of the State]. . . . Vespasian said: "I am now going and will send someone to take my place. You can, however, make a request and I will grant it." Johanan said: "Give me Yavneh and its Wise Men, and the family chain of Rabban of Rabban Gamliel, and physicians to heal Rabbi Zadok." Rabbi Joseph, or some say Rabbi Akiva said [of this request]: "He ought to have said to him: 'Let them [the Jews] off this time.' " He, however, thought that so much he would not grant, and so even a little could not be saved.

How did the physicians heal Rabbi Zadok? The first day they let him drink water in which bran had been soaked; on the next day water in which there had been coarse meal; on the next day water in which there had been flour, so that his stomach expanded little by little.

Vespasian sent Titus who said: "Where is their God the rock in whom they trusted?" [Deut. 33:17] This was the wicked Titus who blasphemed and insulted Heaven. What did he do? He took a harlot by the hand and entered the Holy of Holies and spread out a scroll of the Law and commited a sin on it. He then took a sword and slashed the curtain. . . . Abba Hanan said: "Who is a mighty one like unto You, O Jah? Who is like You in self restraint, that You did hear the blaspheming and insults of that wicked man and keep silent?" In the school of Rabbi Ishmael it was taught: " 'Who is like You among the gods [*elim*]? Who is like You among the dumb ones [*ilmim*]' "

-GITTIN 56A

- 7 -

For three and a half years Vespasian surrounded Jerusalem, having four generals with him: the general of Arabia, of Africa, of Alexandria and of Palestine. . . . There was also Ben Battiah, the nephew of Rabbi Jochanan ben Zakkai, who was appointed in charge of the stores, all of which he burnt. . . . Rabbi Johanan ben Zakkai went out to walk in the market-place and saw how people seethed straw and drank water; and he said to himself, "Can men who seethe straw and drink its water withstand the armies of Vespasian? I must get out of here." He sent a message to Ben Battiah: "Get me out of here." He replied: "We have made an agreement among ourselves that nobody shall leave the city except the dead." He said, "Carry me out in the guise of a corpse." Rabbi Eliezer carried him by the head, Rabbi Joshua by the feet, and Ben Battiah walked in front. When they reached the city gates the guards wanted to stab him. Ben Battiah said to them, "Do you wish people to say that when our teacher died, his body was stabbed!" Speaking to them thus, they allowed him to pass. After going through the gates, they carried him to a cemetery and left him there and returned to the city. Rabbi Johanan ben Zakkai came out and went among the soldiers of Vespasian. He said to them, "Where is the king?" They went and told Vespasian, "A Jew is asking for you." He said to them, "Let him come." On his arrival he exclaimed, "Live, O Lord Emperor!" Vespasian remarked, "You give me a royal greeting but I am not king; and should the king hear of it he will put me to death." He said to him, "If you are not king you will be eventually, because the Temple will only be destroyed by a king." They took him and placed him in the innermost of seven chambers, and asked him what hour of the night it was and he told them. They subsequently asked him what hour of the night it was and he told them. How did Rabbi Johanan ben Zakkai know it? From his study. [i.e. he was accustomed to rehearse his studies and knew how long they took.]

Three days later Vespasian went to take a bath in Gophna. [Jifna, about 15 miles northwest of Jerusalem.] After he had bathed and began dressing, a message arrived and it was announced to him that Nero had died and that the Romans had proclaimed him king. . . . Vespasian said to Rabbi Johanan ben Zakkai, "Make a request of me and I will grant it." He answered, "I beg that you abandon this city of Jerusalem and depart." He said to him, "Did the Romans proclaim me king that I should abandon this city? Make another request of me and I will grant it. He answered, "I beg that you leave the western gate which leads to Lydda, and everyone that departs up to the fourth hour shall be spared." After Vespasian had conquered the city he asked him, "Have you any friends or relatives there? Send and bring him out before the troops enter. He sent Rabbi Eliezer and Rabbi Joshua to bring out Rabbi Zadok. They went and found him in the city gate. When he arrived Rabbi Johanan stood up before him. Vespasian asked, "You stand up before this emaciated old man?" He answered, "By your life, if there had been one more in Jerusalem like him, though you had double your army, you would not have been able to conquer it." . . .

When Vespasian had subdued the city, he assigned the destruction of the four ramparts to the four generals, and the western gate was allotted to Pangar . . . The others demolished their section but he did not demolish his. Vespasian sent for him and asked, "Why did you not destroy your section?" He replied, "By your life, I acted so for the honor of the kingdom; for if I had demolished it, nobody would, in time to come, know what it was you destroyed. . . ."

-MIDRASH LAMENTATIONS RABBAH 5:31

- 8 -

Now, who was this Ben Zakkai? Shall we say, was he then a member of the Sanhedrin? Has it not been taught: The whole lifetime of Rabbi Johanan ben Zakkai was a hundred and twenty years. Forty years he engaged in business, forty years he studied and forty years he taught. And it has also been taught: Forty years before the destruction of the Temple, the Sanhedrin was exiled and took up its residence in Hanuth. This is to teach you that they did not try civil cases. Civil cases? No, they ceased to try capital cases. Again we learnt: When the Temple was destroyed, Rabbi Johanan enacted so and so. But the reference is to some other Ben Zakkai. Reason too supports this; for were Rabbi Johanan ben Zakkai meant, would Rabbi have called him merely Ben Zakkai? . . . He must therefore have been a disciple sitting before his Master, when he made this statement, the reasoning of which was so acceptable to the Sages that they established it in his name. Thus while he was yet a student he was called Ben Zakkai, and when later he was a teacher he was called Johanan ben Zakkai.

-SANHEDRIN 41A

- 9 -

MISHNAH: During the war with Vespasian the Sages decreed against the use of crowns worn by bridegrooms and against the use of the drum. During the war of Quietus they decreed against the use of crowns worn by brides and that nobody should teach his son Greek. During the final war they decreed that a bride should not go out in a palanquin in the midst of the city, but the Sages decreed that a bride may go out in a palanquin in the midst of the city.

When Rabbi Meir died, the composers of fables ceased. When ben Azzai died, the assiduous students of Torah ceased. When Rabbi Akiba died, the glory of Torah ceased. When Rabbi Hanina ben Dosa died, men of deed ceased. When Rabbi Jose Ketanta died, the pious men ceased. When Rabbi Johanan ben Zakkai died, the lustre of Torah ceased. . . .

-SOTAH 49A

- 10 -

Our Sages taught: Once Rabbi Johanan ben Zakkai was riding on an ass when going on a journey, and Rabbi El'azar ben Arak was driving the ass from behind. Rabbi El'azar said to him: "Master, teach me a chapter on the 'Works of the Chariot.' " He answered: "Have I not taught you thus: 'Nor the work of the chariot in the presence of one, unless he is a Sage and understands his own knowledge?' " Rabbi El'azar then said to him: "Master, permit me to say something which you have taught me." He answered: "Say it!" At once Rabbi Johanan ben Zakkai dismounted from the ass, and wrapped himself up [in his prayer shawl] and sat upon a stone beneath an olive tree. Said Rabbi El'azar to him: "Master, why did you dismount?" He answered, "Is it proper that while you are expounding the 'Work of the Chariot' and the Divine Presence is with us, and ministering angels accompany us, I should be riding!" Thereupon Rabbi El'azar ben Arak began to expound the "Work of the Chariot" and fire came down from heaven and encompassed all the trees of the field, and the angels began to utter divine song. . . .

-HAGIGAH 14B

- 11 -

Our Sages taught: Simeon haPakuli arranged the Eighteen Benedictions in order before Rabban Gamliel in Yavneh. Said Rabban Gamliel to the Sages: "Can any one among you frame a benediction relating to the *Minim?*" Samuel the Lesser arose and composed it. The next year he forgot it and tried for two or three hours to recall it, and they did not remove him. Why did they not remove him, seeing that Rabbi Judah has said in the name of Rab: "If a reader made a mistake in any of the other benedictions, they do not remove him, but if [he made a mistake] in the benediction of the *Minim,* he is removed because we suspect him of being a *Min.* Samuel the Lesser is different because he composed it. But is there not a fear that he may have recanted? Abaye said: "We have a tradition that a good man does not become bad." But does he not? Is it not written: "But when the righteous turns away from his righteousness and commits iniquity?" Such a man was originally wicked, but one who was originally righteous does not do so. But is that so? Have we not learnt: "Believe not in yourself until the day of your death?" It is related that Johanan the High Priest officiated as High Priest for eighty years and became a *Min*.

-BERAKHOT 28B

- *12* -

In former times the *lulav* used to be taken to the Temple the entire seven days [of Sukkot] but in the provinces for only one day. After the destruction of the Temple Rabbi Johanan ben Zakkai ordained that the *lulav* should be used in the provinces the entire seven days in remembrance of the Temple . . .

-MISHNAH, SUKKAH 3:12

SUPPLEMENT: CHAPTER SIX

Rabbinic Texts: Eliezer ben Hyrcanus

- 1 -

What was the beginning of Rabbi Eliezer ben Hyrcanus? He was twenty-two years old and had not yet studied Torah. One day he said to his father, "I will go and study Torah with Rabbi Johanan ben Zakkai." His father Hyrcanus replied, "You shall not taste a morsel of food until you shall have plowed a complete furrow." He rose up early in the morning and plowed a complete furrow. It is said that that day was the eve of the Sabbath, so that he went and dined at the house of his father-in-law. Another version is that he tasted nothing between six hours before the Sabbath and six hours after the Sabbath. As he was walking on his way he saw a stone which he thought [to be food]; he took it and put it in his mouth—some say it was cattle dung. He walked on until he came to an inn where he spent the night. He went and sat before Rabban Johanan ben Zakkai in Jerusalem. Soon an offensive smell came forth from his mouth; whereupon Rabban Johanan ben Zakkai said, "Eliezer, my son, have you eaten anything to-day?" He did not answer. Again the question was put to him and he still remained silent. The innkeeper was sent for and asked, "Has Eliezer eaten with you?" He replied, "I thought that perhaps he had eaten at your table, Master." "I too thought that perhaps he had eaten at your table" said Rabban Johanan; "between us we might have lost Rabbi Eliezer." He then said to Rabbi Eliezer, "Just as an offensive smell came forth from your mouth, so shall there go forth from you a distinguished name in Torah." When his father Hyrcanus heard that he was studying Torah under Rabban Johanan ben Zakkai, he declared, "I shall go to Jerusalem and prohibit my son Eliezer by vow from deriving any benefit from my estate." It was said that on that day Rabban Johanan ben Zakkai was sitting and expounding the Torah in Jerusalem, and all the notables of Israel were sitting before him. On learning that Hyrcanus had arrived, he posted watchmen and charged them, "If Hyrcanus comes in and wishes to sit down, do not let him." When he came in and wished to sit down, they did not allow him to do so, and he was compelled to move forward until he came to where Ben Zizith Hakkesheth, Nakdimon ben Gorion, and Ben Kalba Sabua [the richest men in Jerusalem] were seated, and he sat down among them trembling. It was said that on that day Rabban Johanan ben Zakkai turned his gaze upon Rabbi Eliezer and bade him commence the discourse. He said, "I cannot do so." The masters as well as the disciples urged him, whereupon he began the discourse and expounded matters about which no ear had ever heard [the like]. At every utterance that came from his lips, Rabban Johanan ben Zakkai stood up and kissed him on the head; but Rabbi Eliezer exclaimed, "My master, you have taught me the truth." Before the time of adjournment had arrived, his father Hyrcanus stood up and said, "My masters, I came here for the sole purpose of depriving my son Eliezer by vow of my property, but now [I declare] all my property assigned to my son Eliezer, and all his brothers stand dispossessed and deprived of everything."

-ABOTH D'RABBI NATHAN 20B

- 2 -

WHEN TABI HIS SLAVE DIED etc.—Our Rabbis taught: For male and female slaves no row of comforters is formed, nor is the blessing of mourners said, nor is condolence offered. When the bondwoman of Rabbi Eliezer died, his disciples went in to condole with him. When he saw them, he went to an upper chamber, but they went up after him. He then went into an anteroom and they followed him there. He then went into the dining hall and they followed him there. He said to them, "I thought that you would be scalded with warm water; I see you are not scalded even with boiling hot water. Have I not taught you that a row of comforters is not made for male and female slaves, and that a blessing of mourners is not said for them, nor is condolence offered for them? What do they say for them? The same as they say to a man for his ox or for his ass. . . . 'May the Almighty replenish your loss.' "

-BERAKOTH 6B

- 3 -

MISHNA: If a vineyard consists entirely of defective clusters, Rabbi Eliezer says it belongs to the owner, but Rabbi Akiva says, to the poor. . . .

-MISHNAH PE'AH 7:7

- 4 -

Our Rabbis taught: When Rabbi Eliezer was arrested because of *Minuth* [i.e. on suspicion of being a Christian] they brought him to the tribune to be judged. Said the governor to him, "How can a sage man like you occupy himself with idle things?" He replied, "I acknowledge the Judge as right." The governor thought that he referred to him—though he really referred to his Father in Heaven—and said, "Because you have acknowledged me as right, I pardon [you]; you are acquitted." When he came home his disciples called on him to console him, but he would accept no consolation. Said Rabbi Akiba to him, "Master, will you permit me to say one thing of what you have taught me?" He replied, "Say it." "Master," said he, "perhaps some of the teaching of the *Minim* had been transmitted to you and you approved of it, and because of that you were arrested?" He exclaimed, "Akiba you have reminded me! I was once walking in the upper market of Sepphoris when I came across [one of the disciples of Jesus of Nazarene] Jacob of Kfar Sekaniah [Jacob the Little] by name, who said to me: 'it is written in your Torah, *You shall not bring the hire of a harlot . . . into the house of the Lord your God.* [Deut. 23:19] May such money be applied to the erection of a retiring place for the High Priest?' To which I made no reply. Said he to me: 'Thus was I taught by Jesus the Nazarene. *For the hire of a harlot has she gathered them and unto the hire of a harlot shall they return:* [Micah 1:7] they came from a place of filth, let them go to a place of filth.' Those words pleased me very much and that is why I was arrested for apostasy; for in that way I transgressed the scriptural admonition, *Remove you way far from her,*—which refers to *Minuth—and do not come near to the door of her house* [Prov. 5:8]— which refers to the ruling power.

-AVODA ZARA 16B

- 5 -

We learnt elsewhere: If he cut it into separate tiles, placing sand between each tile, Rabbi Eliezer declared it clean and the Sages declared it unclean; and this was the oven of Aknai.

It has been taught: On that day Rabbi Eliezer brought forward every imaginable argument, but they did not accept them. Said he to them, "If the *halakhah* agrees with me let this carob tree prove it!" Thereupon the carob tree was torn a hundred cubits out of its place—others affirm, four hundred cubits. "No proof can be brought from a carob tree," they retorted. Again he said to them: "If the *halakhah* agrees with me, let the stream of water prove it!" Whereupon the stream of water flowed backwards. "No proof can be brought from a stream of water," they rejoined. Again he urged, "If the *halakhah* agrees with me, let the walls of the schoolhouse prove it," whereupon the walls inclined to fall. But Rabbi Joshua rebuked them saying, "When scholars are engaged in *halakhic* debate, why do you interfere?" Hence they did not fall, in honor of Rabbi Joshua, nor did they resume their upright position, in honor of Rabbi Eliezer, and they still stand thus inclined. Again he said to them, "If the *halakhah* agrees with me, let it be proved from Heaven!" Whereupon a Heavenly Voice cried out, "Why do you dispute with Rabbi Eliezer? His decision in all matters of *Halakhah* is correct!" Rabbi Joshua rose up and cried out: *It is not in heaven.* [Deut. 30:12] What did he mean by this? Rabbi Jeremiah said that since the Torah had already been given at Mount Sinai we pay no attention to a Heavenly Voice, for did not God long ago write in the Torah at Mount Sinai, *One must incline after the majority.* [Exodus 23:2]

Rabbi Nathan met Elijah and asked him: "What did the Holy One, Blessed be He, do in that hour?" Elijah replied: "He laughed and said, 'My sons have defeated Me, my sons have defeated Me.'" On that day all objects which Rabbi Eliezer had declared clean were brought and burnt in fire. Then they took a vote and excommunicated him. Said they, "Who shall go and inform him?" "I will go," replied Rabbi Akiba, "lest an unsuitable person go and inform him, and thus destroy the world." What did Rabbi Akiba do? He donned black garments, and wrapped himself in black and sat at a distance of four cubits from him. "Akiba," Rabbi Eliezer said to him, "what has particularly happened today?" "Master," he replied, "it appears to me that your companions hold aloof from you." Thereupon he too tore his garments, took off his shoes and sat on the ground, while tears streamed from his eyes. The world was then smitten: a third of the olive crop, a third of the wheat, and a third of the barley crop. Some say the dough in women's hands swelled up.

-BABA MEZIA 59A

- 6 -

Our Rabbis have taught: It happened that Rabbi Eliezer passed the Sabbath in Upper Galilee, and they asked him for thirty decisions in the laws of *Sukkah*. Of twelve of these he said, "I heard them [from my teachers]"; of eighteen he said, "I have not heard them." Rabbi Jose ben Judah said, "Reverse the words. Of eighteen he said, 'I have heard them,' of twelve he said, 'I have not heard them.' " They said to him, "Are all your words only reproductions of what you have heard?" He answered them, "You wished to force me to say something which I have not heard from my teachers. During all my life . . . no man was earlier than me in the academy. I never slept in the academy. I was always the last to leave, nor did I ever utter profane speech, nor have I ever in my life said a thing which I did not hear from my teachers."

-SUKKA 27B

- 7 -

Our Sages taught: When Rabbi Eliezer fell ill, his disciple went in to visit him. They said to him: "Master, teach us the paths of life so that we may through them win the life of the future world." He said to them: "Be solicitous for the honor of your colleagues, and keep your children from meditation, and set them between the knees of scholars, and when you pray know before whom you are standing, and in this way you will win the future world."

-BERAKHOT 28B

- 8 -

But did not Rabbi Akiba learn from Rabbi Joshua? Surely it has been taught:

When Rabbi Eliezer fell sick, Rabbi Akiba and his companions went to visit him. He was seated in his canopied four-poster while they sat in his bedroom. That day was Sabbath eve, and his son Hyrkanos went in to remove his phylacteries. [ed. note: phylacteries are not worn on the Sabbath]. But his father rebuked him, and he departed crestfallen. "It seems to me," said he to them "that my father's mind is deranged." But Rabbi Akiba said to him: "His mind is clear, you mother's is deranged. How can one neglect a prohibition which is punished by death and turn his attention to something which is merely forbidden as a *shebuth*?" [ed. note: Rabbi Eliezer had noticed that his wife had not yet kindled the Sabbath lights nor put away the Sabbath meal to keep it hot. Both of these, if done on the Sabbath are punishable by stoning, whereas the wearing of phylacteries indoors is forbidden merely by a Rabbinical ordinance, lest one forget himself and go out in the street with them, which is biblically forbidden.]

The Sages, seeing that his mind was clear, entered his chamber and sat down at a distance of four cubits. "Why have you come?" said he to them. "To study the Torah," they replied. "And why did you not come before now?" he asked. They answered, "We had no time." He then said "I will be surprised if these die a natural death." Rabbi Akiba asked him, "And what will my death be?" and he answered, "Yours will be more cruel than theirs." He then put his two arms over his heart and bewailed them, saying, "Woe to you, two arms of mine, that have been like two scrolls of the Torah that are wrapped up. Much Torah have I studied and much have I taught. Much Torah have I learnt, yet have I but skimmed from the knowledge of my teachers as much as a dog lapping from the sea. Much Torah have I taught, yet my disciples have only drawn from me as much as a painting stick from its tube. Moreover, I have studied three hundred laws on the subject of a deep bright spot [ed. note: one of the forms of leprosy, cf Lev.12:2], yet no man has ever asked me about them.

Moreover, I have studied three hundred [or as others state, three thousand] laws about the planting of cucumbers by magic, and no man, except Akiba ben Joseph ever questioned me about it. For once it happened that he and I were walking together on a road, when he said to me, 'My master, teach me about the planting of cucumbers.' I made one statement and the whole field was filled with cucumbers. Then he said, 'Master, you have taught me how to plant them. Now teach me how to gather them up.' I said something, and all the cucumbers gathered in one place."

His visitors then asked him, "What is the law of a ball, a shoemaker's last, an amulet, a leather bag containing pearls and a small weight?" He replied, "They can become unclean, and if unclean, they are restored to their uncleanliness just as they are." Then they asked him, "What of a shoe that is on the last?" "It is clean," and in pronouncing this word his soul departed. Then Rabbi Joshua arose and exclaimed, "The vow is annulled, the vow is annulled!" On the conclusion of the Sabbath Rabbi Akiba met his bier being carried from Caesarea to Lydda . . . Then Rabbi Akiba commenced his funeral address, the mourners being lined up about the coffin, and said: "*My father, my father, the chariot of Israel and the horsemen thereof* [2 Kings 2:12]; I have many coins but no money changer to accept them. . . ."

SUPPLEMENT: CHAPTER SIX

Rabbinic Texts: Joshua ben Hananiah

- 1 -

Rabbi Hanina ben Ida said: Why are the words of Torah likened unto water—as it is written, *Ho, everyone that thirsteth come ye for water*? [Isa. 55:1] This is to teach you, just as water flows from a higher level to a lower, so too the words of Torah endure only with him who is meek-minded. Rabbi Oshaia said: Why are the words of Torah likened unto these three liquids, water, wine and milk—as it is written, *Ho, everyone that thirsteth come ye for water*, and it is written, *Come ye and buy and eat, yea come buy wine and milk without money and without price*? This is to teach you, just as these three liquids can only be preserved in the most inferior vessels, so too the words of Torah endure only with him who is meek-minded. This is illustrated by the story of the daughter of the Emperor [Hadrian] who addressed Rabbi Joshua ben Hananiah, "O glorious wisdom in an ugly vessel!" He replied, "Does not your father keep wine in an earthenware vessel?" She asked, "In what else shall he keep it?" He said to her, "You who are nobles should keep it in vessels of gold and silver." Thereupon she went and told it to her father and he had the wine put in vessels of gold and silver, and it became sour. When he was informed of this he asked his daughter, "Who gave you this advice?" She replied, "Rabbi Joshua ben Hananiah." Thereupon the Emperor had him summoned before him and asked him, "why did you give her such advice?" He replied, "I answered her according to the way she spoke to me." But are there not good looking people

who are learned?—If these people were ugly they would be still
more learned.

- 2 -

In the days of Rabbi Joshua ben Hananiah the [Roman] State
ordered the Temple to be rebuilt. Pappus and Lulianus set tables
from Acco as far as Antioch and provided those who came up
from exile [i.e. from Babylon] with all their needs. Whereupon
Samaritans went and warned the Emperor, "Let the King be
aware that if this rebellious city is rebuilt and the walls finished,
they will declare their independence!" The Emperor replied,
"Yet what can I do, seeing that I have already given the order?"
They replied, "Issue an order that they must change its site, or
add five cubits to it, or lessen it by five cubits, and they will
withdraw of their own accord." Now the Community [of Israel]
was assembled in the plain of Beth Rimmon. When the [royal]
dispatches arrived, they burst out weeping, and wanted to revolt
against the [Roman] power. Hearing this the Sages decided: "Let
a wise man go and pacify the congregation, and let that man be
Joshua ben Hananiah. He is a master of Scripture [and a persuasive speaker]." So Joshua went and delivered an eloquent and
convincing plea. This is what he said: "A wild lion killed an
animal, and a bone stuck in his throat. Thereupon he proclaimed: 'I will reward any one who removes it.' An Egyptian
heron, which has a long beak, came and pulled it out and demanded his reward. 'Go,' replied the lion, 'you will be able to
boast that you entered the lion's mouth in peace and came out in
peace.' Even so, let us be satisfied that we entered into dealings
with this people in peace and have emerged in peace."

-MIDRASH, GENESIS RABBAH 64:10

- *3* -

Rabbi Joshua ben Hananiah remarked: No one has ever had the better of me except a woman, a little boy and a little girl. What was the incident with the woman? I was staying at an inn where the hostess served me with beans. On the first day I ate all of them, leaving nothing. On the second day too I left nothing. On the third day she over seasoned them with salt, and as soon as I tasted them, I withdrew my hand. "My Master," she said to me, "why did you not eat?" "I have already eaten earlier in the day," I replied . . . "My master," she said, "Is it possible that you left [the dish today] as compensation for the former meals, for have not the Sages stated: 'Nothing is to be left in the pot, but something must be left on the plate?' " What was the incident with the little girl? I was once on a journey and observing a path across a field, I made my way through it, when a little girl called out to me, "Master! Is not this part of the field?" "No," I replied, "this is a trodden path." "Robbers like yourself," she retorted, "have trodden it down!" What was the incident with the little boy? I was once on a journey when I noticed a little boy sitting at a cross-road. "By what road," I asked him, "do we go to town?" "This one," he replied, "is short but long and that one is long but short." I proceeded along the "short but long" road. When I approached the town I discovered that it was hedged in by gardens and orchards. Turning back I said to him, "My son, did you not tell me that the road was short?" "And," he replied, "did I not also tell you 'but long' "? I kissed him upon the head and said to him, "Happy are you, O Israel, all of you are wise, both young and old."

-ERUBIN 53A

- *4* -

Rabbi Joshua ben Hananiah was once at the court of Hadrian. A certain *Min* [probably an early Christian] said to him through gestures: "You are a people whose Lord has turned his face from them." In reply, Rabbi Joshua made gestures to retort: "His hand is stretched out over us." Said Hadrian to Rabbi Joshua, "What did his gestures signify?" "He was saying that we are a people from whom the Lord has turned His face, and my reply was that God's hand is stretched out over us. . . ."

When the time of Rabbi Joshua's death approached, the Sages said to him: "What will become of us at the hands of the unbelievers?" He answered them: *Counsel is perished from the prudent, their wisdom is vanished* [Jer. 49:7] So soon as counsel is perished from the prudent, the wisdom of the peoples of the world is vanished." [i.e. the polemics of the unbelievers will cease]

-HAGIGAH 5B

- 5 -

It was taught: Rabbi Joshua ben Hananiah stated, "When we used to rejoice at the place of the Water-Drawing, our eyes saw no sleep. How was this? The first hour was occupied with daily morning sacrifice; from there we proceeded to prayers, from there we proceeded to the additional service, then to the House of Study, then the eating and drinking, then the afternoon prayer, then the evening sacrifice, and after that rejoicing at the place of the Water Drawing all night. . . ."

-SUKKAH 53A

- 6 -

The Emperor once said to Rabbi Joshua ben Hananiah: "Your God is likened to a lion, for it is written *The lion has roared, who will not fear? The Lord God has spoken, who can but prophesy?* [Amos

3:8] But what is the greatness of this? A horseman can kill a lion!" He replied, "God has not been likened to an ordinary lion of Be-Illai'i." "I want you to show it to me," said the Emperor. "It is impossible for you to see," was his reply. "Indeed," said the Emperor, "I *will* see it." So Rabbi Joshua prayed and the lion set out from its place. When it was four hundred parasangs away it roared once, and all pregnant women miscarried and the walls of Rome fell. When it was three hundred parasangs distant it roared again and people's teeth fell out; even the Emperor himself fell from his throne to the ground. "Please," he begged of Joshua, "pray that it return to its place." He prayed and it returned to its place.

Another time the Emperor said to Rabbi Joshua ben Hananiah, "I wish to see your God." He replied, "You cannot see Him." "Indeed," said the Emperor, "I *will* see Him." He went and place the Emperor facing the sun during the summer solstice and said to him, "Look up at it." He replied, "I cannot." Said Rabbi Joshua, "If you cannot look at the sun, which is only one of the servants that attend the Holy One, blessed be He, how can you presume to look upon the divine Presence?"

On another occasion the Emperor said to Rabbi Joshua ben Hananiah, "I wish to prepare a banquet for your God." He replied, "You could not undertake it." "Why?" "Because his attendants are too numerous." "Indeed, I will do it," the Emperor persisted. "Then" said Joshua, "go and prepare it on the spacious banks of the Great Sea." The Emperor spent six months of summer in making preparations when rain fell and washed everything into the sea. "What is the meaning of this?" asked the Emperor. "They are but the sweepers and sprinklers that march before Him!" was the reply. "In that case," said the Emperor, "I cannot do it."

The Emperor's daughter once said to Rabbi Joshua ben Hananiah, "Your God is a carpenter, for it is written, *Who layeth the beams of His upper chambers in the waters.* Ask Him to make me a spool." He replied, "Very well." He prayed for her and she was smitten with leprosy. She was then removed to the open square of Rome and given a spool. [For so it was the custom in Rome, whoever was smitten with leprosy was given a spool and removed to the open square, and was given skeins to wind, so that people may see them and pray for their recovery.] One day as Rabbi Joshua was passing he saw her sitting in the open square of Rome and winding the skeins on the spool. He remarked, "My God has given you a beautiful spool." She said, "I pray you, ask your God to take back what He has given me. . . ."

-HULLIN 59B

- 7 -

A Tanna taught: *Eduyyoth* [a tractate of the Talmud dealing with testimony in court] was formulated on that day—and wherever the expression 'on that day' is used, it refers to *that* day—and there was no *halakhah* about which any doubt existed in the *Beth haMidrash* which was not fully elucidated. Rabban Gamliel also did not absent himself from the *Beth ha Midrash* a single hour, as we have learnt: On that day, Judah an Ammonite proselyte, came before them in the *Beth haMidrash*. He said to them, "Am I permitted to enter the assembly?" Rabbi Joshua said to him, "You are permitted to enter the congregation." Said Rabban Gamliel to him, "Is it not already laid down that *An Ammonite or a Moabite may not enter in the assembly of the Lord*?" [Deut.23:4] Rabbi Joshua replied to him, "Do Ammon and Moab still reside in their original homes? Sennacherib king of Assyria long ago went up and mixed up all the nations, as it says, *I have erased the borders of peoples; I have plundered their treasures, and exiled their vast populations* [Isa. 10:13] and whatever strays from a group is assumed to belong to the larger sections of the group." [i.e. since the Ammonites were scattered among a majority of other peoples, one may deduce that this man is not really an Ammonite!] Said Rabban Gamliel to him, "But has it not been said, *Afterwards I will restore the fortunes of the Ammonite, declares the Lord* [Jer. 49:6], so they have already returned." To which Rabbi Joshua replied, "And has it not been

said, *I will restore my people Israel* and they have not yet returned?"
Immediately they permitted him to enter the congregation.
[Note: This debate is evidence of missionary activity within Rabbinic Judaism.] Rabban Gamliel then said, "This being the case I
will go and apologize to Rabbi Joshua." When he reached his
house he saw that the walls were black. He said to him, "From the
walls of your house it is apparent that you are a charcoal-burner."
Joshua replied, "Alas for the generations of which you are the
leader, seeing that you know nothing of the troubles of the scholars, their struggles to support and sustain themselves!" He said to
him, "I apologize, forgive me." He paid no attention to him. "Do
it," said Rabban Gamliel, "out of respect for my father." He then
became reconciled to him. . . .

-BERAKHOT 28A

SUPPLEMENT: CHAPTER SEVEN

Rabbinic Texts: Akiba ben Joseph

- 1 -

Rab Judah said in the name of Rab: When Moses ascended on high he found the Holy One, blessed be He, engaged in affixing coronets to the letters [of the Torah]. Said Moses, "Lord of the Universe, who holds you back?" [i.e. is there anything wanting in the Torah that these additions are necessary?] He answered, "There will arise a man at the end of many generations, Akiba ben Joseph by name, who will expound on each tittle heaps and heaps of laws." "Lord of the universe," said Moses, "permit me to see him." He replied, "Turn around." Moses went and sat down behind eight rows [of Akiba's disciples] and listened to the discourses upon the law. Not being able to follow their arguments, he was ill at ease, but when they came to a certain subject and the disciples said to the Master, "From where do you derive this?", Akiba replied, "It is the law given unto Moses at Sinai" he was comforted. Thereupon he returned to the Holy One, blessed be He, and said: "Lord of the Universe, you have such a man, and you give the Torah through me?" God replied, "Be silent, for such is My decree!" Then said Moses, "Lord of the Universe, You have shown me his Torah, now show me his reward." "Turn around," said God. Moses turned around and saw them weighing out his flesh at the market stalls. "Lord of the Universe," cried Moses, "such Torah and such a reward!" God replied, "Be silent, for such is My decree!"

-MENAHOT 29B

176

- 2 -

What was the beginning of Rabbi Akiba? It was said of him that at the age of forty he had learnt nothing at all. On one occasion, as he was standing by the mouth of a well, he inquired, "Who carved out this stone?" They answered, "The water which constantly falls on it, day in day out." They continued, "Akiba, have you not read the verse, *The waters wear the stones* [Job 14:19]?" Forthwith Rabbi Akiba applied to himself the following *a fortiori* argument: If the soft water can wear away the hard stone, how much more can the words of the Torah, which are hard like iron, carve a way into my heart which is of flesh and blood! Immediately he turned to the study of Torah. Both he and his son went and sat down before the schoolteacher and said to him, "Master, teach us Torah." Rabbi Akiba took hold of the tablet by one hand, and his son by the other end, and on it the teacher wrote *'alef beth* which he learnt, *'alef taw* which he learnt, and then the book of Leviticus which he also learnt. So he continued to study until he had learnt the whole Torah. He then went and sat before Rabbi Eliezer and Rabbi Joshua and said to them, "My Masters, initiate me into the reasoning of the Mishnah." As soon as they recited one *halakhah* to him, he went away and sat down alone asking himself, "Why is *'alef* so written, why is *beth* so written? Why is this stated?" He thereupon returned to his masters and asked them, and held them up with his words.

Rabbi Simeon ben Eleazer said: I will illustrate this to you by a parable. To what can this be compared? To a stonemason who is quarrying stones in a mountain. One day he took his pick in his hand, went out and sat on the mountain, and chipped away small stones. When people came and asked him what he was doing, he told them, "I mean to uproot the mountain and cast it into the Jordan." They said to him, "You cannot possibly uproot the whole mountain." Nevertheless he continued chipping away until it became the size of a large boulder. He inserted himself beneath it, unloosed it, uprooted it, and cast it into the Jordan, saying, "Here is not your place, but there." Thus Rabbi Akiba gleaned the knowledge of Torah from Rabbi Eliezer and Rabbi Joshua. Rabbi Tarfon said to him, "Akiba, it is of you that the verse speaks, *He dams up the sources of the streams so that hidden things may be brought to light.* [Job 28:11] Rabbi Akiba brought to light the things that were hidden from all others.

Every day he used to gather a bundle of wood, half of which he sold to provide food for himself, and the other half he used for his personal needs. His neighbors rose up against him and cried, "Akiba, you are ruining us with your smoke! Come and sell all the wood to us, and with the money you can buy oil and study by the light of an oil lamp." But he replied, "I derive many uses from the wood: first I study by its light, secondly I keep myself warm by it, and thirdly I am able to sleep on it."

In the Hereafter the example of Rabbi Akiba will condemn all the poor; for when they will be charged, "Why did you not study Torah?" and they plead, "Because we were too poor," the reply will be given, "Was not Rabbi Akiba very poor and in the most difficult circumstances?" And if they plead, "Because of our little children" they will be told, "Did not Rabbi Akiba have many sons and daughters for whom he had to provide, as well as his wife Rachel. He was forty years old when he started to study Torah, and by the end of thirteen years he taught Torah in public. It is said that he did not depart this life before he had enjoyed the luxury tables of silver and gold, and ascended his bed by golden steps. His wife went out dressed in fine robes and wearing a golden tiara. When his disciples said to him, Master, you put us to shame by the lavish way you treat her," he replied, "Much hardship has she endured with me for the sake of the Torah."

-ABOTH D'RABBI NATHAN 20B

- 3 -

Rabbi Akiba was a shepherd of Kalba Sabua. The latter's daughter, seeing how modest and noble he was, said to him, "Were I to be betrothed to you, would you go away to study at an academy?" "Yes," he replied. She then became secretly betrothed to him and sent him away. When her father heard what she had done he drove her from his house and disinherited her. Rabbi Akiba departed and spent twelve years at the academy. When he returned home he brought with him twelve thousand disciples. While in his home town he heard an old man saying to her, "How long will you lead the life of a living widowhood?" "If he would listen to me," she replied, "he would spend another twelve years in study." Said Rabbi Akiba, "It is then with her consent that I am acting," and he departed again and spent another twelve years at the academy. When he finally returned he brought with him twenty-four thousand disciples. His wife heard of his arrival and went out to meet him, when her neighbors said to her, "Borrow some respectable clothes and put them on," but she replied: *A righteous man knows the needs of his beast* [Prov. 12:10]. On approaching him she fell upon her face and kissed his feet. His attendants were about to thrust her aside, when Rabbi Akiba cried to them, "Leave her alone. Mine and yours are hers." Her father, on hearing that a great man had come to town said: "I will go and perhaps he will invalidate my vow." [note: which he had made to disinherit his daughter] When he came to him, Rabbi Akiba asked, "Would you have made your vow if you had known he was a great man?" "Had he known," the other replied, "even one chapter or even one single *halakhah*, I would not have made the vow." Akiba then said to him, "I am the man." The other fell on his face and kissed his feet and also gave him half of his wealth.

-KETUBOT 62B

- *4* -

Long ago, as Rabban Gamliel, Rabbi El'azar ben Azariah, Rabbi Joshua and Rabbi Akiba were walking on the road, they heard the noise of the crowds at Rome on traveling from Puteoli, a hundred and twenty miles away. They all began to weep, but Rabbi Akiba seemed joyful. They said to him, "Why are you joyful?" He replied, "Why are you weeping?" They answered,

"These heathens who bow down to images and burn incense to idols live in safety and ease, whereas our Temple, the 'Footstool' of our God [Ps.99:5] is burnt down by fire, and should we then not weep?" He replied, "That is precisely the reason I am joyful, for if they that offend Him fare thus, how much better shall they fare who obey Him!" On another occasion they were coming up to Jerusalem together, and just as they came to Mount Scopus they saw a fox emerging from the Holy of Holies. They began to weep, and Rabbi Akiba seemed joyful. "Why," they said to him, "are you joyful?" He retorted, "And why are you weeping?" Said they to him, "A place of which it was once said, *Any outsider who encroaches shall be put to death* [Nu. 1:51] has become the haunt of foxes, and should we not weep?" He said to them, "That is exactly why I am joyful; for it is written, *and call reliable witnesses, the priest Uriah and Zechariah son of Jeberechiah, to witness for me* [Isa. 8:2]. Now what is the connection between Uriah and Zechariah? Uriah lived during the time of the first Temple, while Zechariah lived [and prophesied] during the second Temple; but Scripture linked the later prophesy of Zechariah with the earlier prophesy of Uriah. In the earlier prophesy of Uriah it is written, *Zion shall be plowed as a field, Jerusalem shall become a heap of ruins* [Jer. 26:18]. In Zechariah it is written, *There shall yet be old men and women in the squares of Jerusalem.* [Zech. 8:4] Now as long as Uriah's threatening prophesy had not been fulfilled, I was afraid that Zechariah's optimistic message would not be fulfilled. Now, however, since Uriah's dire prediction has been literally fulfilled, it is quite certain that Zechariah's prophesy will also find its literal fulfillment." Said they to him, "Akiba you have comforted us! Akiba you have comforted us!"

-MAKKOTH 24B

- *5* -

Our Sages taught: Four men entered *Pardes* [lit. 'Garden,' a term signifying mystical studies] namely, Ben 'Azzai, and Ben Zoma,

Aher [i.e. Elisha ben Abuya] and Rabbi Akiba. Rabbi Akiba said to them, "When you arrive at the stones of pure marble, do not say 'Water, water!' For it is said, *He who deals deceitfully shall not live in my house.*" [Ps. 101:7] Ben 'Azzai cast a look and died. Of him Scripture says, *The death of his faithful ones is grievous in the Lord's sight.* [Ps.116:15] Ben Zoma looked and became demented. Of him Scripture says, *If you find honey, eat only what you need, lest, surfeiting yourself, you throw it up.* [Prov. 25:16] Aher mutilated the shoots. [i.e. apostasized—cf. Chapter 8] Rabbi Akiba departed unhurt.

-HAGIGAH 14B

- 6 -

Rabbi Joshua ben Karha said: "Whoever studies the Torah and does not revise it is likened to one who sows without reaping." Rabbi Joshua said: "He who studies the Torah and forgets it is like a woman who bears a child and buries it." Rabbi Akiba said: "Chant it every day, chant it every day." Said Rabbi Isaac ben Abdimi: "What verse supports this?—*The appetite of a laborer labors for him, because his hunger forces him on* [Prov. 16:26] he toils in one place, the Torah toils for him in another." [i.e. as a reward for repeated revision, Torah ensures a complete remembrance and understanding.]

-SANHEDRIN 99A

- 7 -

Rabbi Akiba said: A fence to honor is the avoidance of jesting, a fence of wisdom is silence, a fence to vows is self-restraint, a fence to purity is holiness, a fence to humility is the fear of sin.

He used to say: Do not associate with scoffers lest you learn their ways. Do not eat bread with a priest who is an ignoramus, lest you trespass in hallowed things. Do not make vows readily, lest you trespass in oaths. Do not be in the habit of feasting sumptuously, lest in the end you will have to eat the bread of charity. Do not bring yourself into a state of doubt lest you come up against certain transgression. Do not leave the Land of Israel, lest you serve idols . . .

He used to say: Whoever is buried in other lands is considered as though he were buried in Babylon; whoever is buried in Babylon is as though he were buried in the Land of Israel; whoever is buried in the Land of Israel is as though he were buried beneath the altar; and whoever is buried beneath the altar is as though he were buried beneath the Throne of Glory . . .

He used to say: An ignorant man cannot be pious, the bashful man cannot learn and the impatient man cannot teach. He used to say: Why do disciples of the Sages die young? It is not because they are immoral or because they rob; but because they interrupt their study of Torah to indulge in idle talk. Moreover, when returning to their studies they do not begin where they left off . . .

—ABOTH D'RABBI NATHAN 27B

- *8* -

Rabbi Huna said in the name of Rab citing Rabbi Meir, and so it was taught in the name of Rabbi Akiba: One should always accustom himself to say, "Whatever the All-Merciful does is for good." This is exemplified by the following incident: Rabbi Akiba was once traveling along a certain road and he came to a town where he looked for lodging but was turned down everywhere. He said, "Whatever the All-Merciful does is for good," and he went and spent the night in the open field. He had with him a cock, an ass and a lamp. A gust of wind came and blew out the lamp; a weasel came and ate the cock; a lion came and ate the ass. He said:

"Whatever the All-Merciful does is for the good." The same night, some brigands came and carried off all the inhabitants of the town. He said: "Did I not say to you that whatever the All-Merciful does is for good?"

-BERAKHOT 60B

- 9 -

It was said that Rabbi Akiba had twelve thousand pairs of disciples, from Gabbatha to Antipatris; and all of them died at the same time because they did not treat each other with respect. The world remained desolate until Rabbi Akiba came to our Masters in the South and taught Torah to them. These were Rabbi Meir, Rabbi Judah, Rabbi Jose, Rabbi Simeon and Rabbi Eleazar ben Shammua; and it was they who revived the Torah at that time. A Tanna taught: All of them died between Passover and Shavuot. Rabbi Hamma ben Abba or, it might be said Rabbi Hiyya ben Abin said: All of them died a cruel death. [i.e. during the Hadrianic persecutions]

-YEBAMOT 62B

- 10 -

Five things did Rabbi Akiba charge Rabbi Simeon bar Yohai when he was immured in prison. Simeon said to him, "Master, teach me Torah." "I will not teach you," he replied. "If you do not teach me," said he, "I will tell my father Yohai and he will deliver you to the State." "My son" he answered, "more than the calf wished to suck does the cow desire to suckle." Said Simeon to him, "Yet who is in danger? Surely the calf is in danger!" Said he to him, "If you wish to be strangled, be hanged on a large tree [i.e. if you want to depend on authority, see that it is a great one], and when you teach your son, teach him from a corrected scroll. Do not cook in a pot in which your neighbor has cooked [i.e. do not marry a divorced woman in her husband's lifetime]."

-PESAHIM 112A

- 11 -

Our Rabbis taught: Rabbi Akiba was once confined in a prison house and Rabbi Joshua the grits-maker was attending on him. Every day a certain quantity of water was brought in to him. On one occasion he was met by the prison keeper who said to him, "You appear to have more water than you need. Do you perhaps intend to use it to undermine the prison?" He poured out half of it and handed him the other half. When he came to Rabbi Akiba the latter said to him, "Joshua, do you not know that I am an old man and my life depends on yours?" When the latter told him all that had happened Rabbi Akiba said to him, "Give me some water to wash my hands." "It will not be enough for drinking," the other complained, "will it be enough for washing your hands?" "What can I do," the former replied, "when for neglecting the words of the Sages [who ordained the washing of hands before eating] one deserves death? It is better that I myself should die than that I should transgress against the opinion of my colleagues." It was related that he tasted nothing until the other had brought him water with which to wash his hands. When the Sages heard of this incident they remarked, "If he was so scrupulous in his old age how much more must he have been so in his youth; if he behaved thus in prison, how much more had he behaved thus when free!"

-ERUBIM 21B

- 12 -

MISHNAH: If *halizah* is performed with two or three, and one turns out to be a kinsman or ineligible, the *halizah* is invalid.

Rabbi Simeon and Rabbi Johanan the Cobbler declare it valid. It happened that *halizah* was performed between the woman and the man in prison, and the case came before Rabbi Akiba and he declared it valid. GEMARA: It took place in prison. And it was brought before him in prison.

-JERUSALEM TALMUD, YEBAMOT 12:5*

- 13 -

One may not intercalate more than one year at a time. If it is done, it is not valid, for you may not intercalate more than one year at a time. Rabbi Simeon permits it. He cited an instance when Rabbi Akiba was in prison and, he intercalated three successive years at one time.

-TOSEFTA SANHEDRIN, 2:8*

- 14 -

One who has had a nocturnal emission and has no ritual bath available in which to immerse himself must say the *Shema* inaudibly, according to Rabbi Meir. But the Sages rule that he may say the Shema audibly, and the blessings that precede and follow it as well. Rabbi Meir said: "Once we were sitting and studying with Rabbi Akiba, and we said the *Shema* inaudibly because a guard stood at the door."

-TOSEFTA, BERAKHOT 2:13*

- 15 -

Rabbi Hiyya bar Abba said: If one should say to me, "Sacrifice your life for the sanctification of God's name," I am ready to do so on condition they slay me at once. What did they used to do on the generation of the Great Persecution [in the days of Hadrian]? They brought iron discs and made them red hot and put them under their armpits until they expired. Or they brought needles and stuck them under their nails until they expired. When Rabbi Akiba was in prison for two years they brought needles and stuck them under his nails, hot iron discs and stuck them under his armpits.

-MIDRASH, SONG OF SONGS RABBAH 2:7*

- 16 -

In the time of proscription the following *halakhah* was inquired for: If a minor left her first husband by divorce and her second husband by annulment, may she return to her first husband? They hired a man for four hundred zuz and through him they addressed the inquiry to Rabbi Akiba in prison, and he stated she was forbidden. . . .

-YEBAMOT 108B

- 17 -

The question was raised: Did it happen that *halizah* was performed privately outside, and the case was brought to Rabbi Akiba in prison, or perhaps the *halizah* . . . was performed in prison? Rab Judah replied in the name of Rab: The incident occurred in prison and the case also came up for decision in prison.

-YEBAMOT 105B

- *18* -

Our Sages taught: Once the wicked government issued a decree forbidding the Jews to study and practice the Torah. Pappus ben Judah came and found Rabbi Akiba publicly bringing gatherings together and occupying himself with the Torah. He said to him, "Akiba, are you not afraid of the government?" He replied, "I will explain to you with a parable. A fox was once walking alongside a river, and he saw fish going in swarms from one place to another. He said to them, 'From what are you fleeing?' They replied, 'From the nets cast for us by men.' He said to them, 'Would you like to come up on dry land so that you and I can live together in the way my ancestors lived with your ancestors?' They replied, 'And people say you are the cleverest of creatures. You are the most stupid. For if we are in danger in our natural environment, where we live, how much more so would it be outside it, where we would die. So it is with us. If such is our condition when we sit and study the Torah, of which it is written, *For therefore you shall have life and long endure* [Deut.30:20]; if we neglect it how much worse off shall we be!" It is related that soon afterwards Rabbi Akiba was arrested, and Pappus ben Judah was also arrested and imprisoned next to him. He said to him, "Pappus, who brought you here?" He replied, "Happy are you, Rabbi Akiba, that you have been seized for busying yourself with the Torah! Alas for Pappus who has been seized for busying himself with idle things!" When Rabbi Akiba was taken out for execution, it was the hour for the recital of the *Shema,* and while they combed his flesh with iron combs, he was accepting upon himself the kingship of heaven. His disciples said to him, "Our Teacher, even to this point?" He said to them, "All my days I have been troubled by this verse, *with all my soul* [Deut. 6:5], which I interpret to mean even if He takes my soul. I said, 'When shall I have the opportunity of fulfilling this?' Now that I have the opportunity shall I not fulfill it?" He prolonged the word *ehad* until he expired while saying it. A *bath kol* went forth and proclaimed, "Happy are you, Akiba, that your soul has departed with the word *ehad!*" The ministering angels said before the Holy One blessed be He, "Such Torah and such a reward? He should have been *from them that die by Your hand, O Lord.* [Ps. 19:14] God replied to them, *their portion is in life.* [ibid.] A *bath kpl* went forth and proclaimed, "Happy are you, Rabbi Akiba, that you are destined for the life of the world to come!"

-BERAKHOT 61B

SUPPLEMENT: CHAPTER EIGHT

Rabbinic Texts: Rabbi Meir

- 1 -

The story is told about Rabbi Meir that he was once sitting and expounding in the Synagogue on Sabbath afternoon, during the afternoon prayers, and while he was doing this his two sons died. What did their mother [Beruriah] do? She placed the two of them on a bed and covered them with a sheet.

When the Sabbath was concluded, Rabbi Meir came home from the House of Study. He said to her, "Where are my two sons?" She answered, "They went to the House of Study." Said he, "I looked for them at the House of Study, and I did not see them." She then gave him the *havdalah* cup and he made the *havdalah* blessings, and again he asked her, "Where are my two sons?" She replied, "They went to such-and-such a place, and they will return soon." She then served him his dinner. After he finished eating she said to him, "I have a question to ask you." He said to her, "Ask." She said, "Just a little while ago a man left me a pledge to keep for him. He has now returned and wants it back. Shall I give it to him." He replied, "My beloved, is not he who holds a pledge required to return it to its rightful owner?" Said she: "Were it not for your opinion, I would not have returned it."

What did she do? She took him by the hand, led him to the room and brought him right up to the bed. He began to weep and cried out, "My sons! My sons! My teachers! My sons in the ways of the world, and my teachers who brightened my eyes with their Torah!"

At that moment she said to him, "Meir, did you not say yourself that we must return the pledge to its owner? The Lord has given, the Lord has taken away, blessed be the Name of the Lord."

-MIDRASH TO PROVERBS, IN *SEFER AGADA,*
H.N. BIALIK, VOL.2 P.190*

- 2 -

Northward [*zafona*] *before the Lord* [Lev. 1:11] refers to the deeds of Abraham, Isaac and Jacob which are treasured up [zefunim] with Him. Whence do we know that this word is an expression meaning the laying up of treasure? Since it is said, *New and old have I laid up* [*zafanti*] *for thee, O beloved.* [Song of Songs 7:14] Abraham, Isaac and Jacob are meant by "old ones," Amram, son of Kohath, and all the worthy men who were in Egypt are meant by "new ones," as it is said *New and old etc.* Others say, the company of Moses, the company of Joshua, the company of David and Hezekiah are meant by "old ones," while the companies of Ezra, Hillel, Rabbi Johanan ben Zakkai and Rabbi Meir and his colleagues are meant by "new ones."

-MIDRASH, LEVITICUS RABBAH 2:11*

- 3 -

Rabbi Akiba appointed Rabbi Meir and Rabbi Simeon. He said, "Let Rabbi Meir be first." Whereupon Rabbi Simeon became

downcast. Said Rabbi Akiba to him, "By your life! Both I and
your Creator recognize your talents."

-JERUSALEM TALMUD, SANHEDRIN 19A*

- 4 -

Rabbi Meir related, "When I was with Rabbi Akiba I used to put
vitriol into my ink and he told me nothing against it. However,
when I subsequently came to Rabbi Ishmael, the latter said to
me, "What is your occupation?" I told him that I was a scribe. He
said to me, "Be meticulous in your work, your occupation is a
sacred one."

-ERUVIN 13A

- 5 -

In the copy of Rabbi Meir's Torah it was found written *And behold
it was very good.* [*tov m'od*] [Gen. 1:31], "behold death is good [*tov
mot*]." Rabbi Samuel ben Nahmani said, "I was seated on my
grandfather's shoulder going up from my town to Kfar Hana via
Bet She'an and I heard Rabbi Simeon ben Eleazer say in Rabbi
Meir's name *"And behold it was very good*—behold death is good."

-MIDRASH GENESIS RABBAH 9:5

- 6 -

Rabbi Huna said in the name of Rabbi Meir: A man's words
should always be few in addressing the Holy One, Praised be He
since it says, *Keep your mouth from being rash, and let not your lips be*

quick to bring forth speech before God. For God is in heaven and you are on earth; that is why your words should be few. [Eccl. 5:1]

- 7 -

Rabbi Jose the Galilean was once on a journey when he met Beruriah [Meir's wife]. "By what road," he asked, "do we go to Lydda?" "Foolish Galilean," she replied, "did not the Sages forbid you to talk at length with women? You should have asked, 'Lydda?'

Beruriah once discovered a student who was studying in a low voice. Rebuking him, she exclaimed, "Is it not written, *Ordered in all things and sure?* [2 Sam. 23:5] If it is ordered in your 248 limbs, it will be sure, otherwise it will not be sure."

-ERUBIN 53A

- 8 -

They brought up Rabbi Haninah ben Teradion and asked him, "Why have you occupied yourself with the Torah?" He replied, "The Lord my God has commanded me to do this." At once they [the Romans] sentenced him to be burnt, his wife to be slain, and his daughter to be consigned to a brothel.

It was said that within a few days Rabbi Jose ben Kisma died and all the great men of Rome went to the burial and made great lamentation for him. On their return, they found Rabbi Haninah ben Teradion sitting and occupying himself with the Torah, publicly gathering assemblies, and keeping a scroll of the Torah in his bosom. Straightaway they took hold of him, wrapped him in the Scroll of the Torah, placed bundles of branches around him and set them on fire. They then brought tufts of wool, which they had soaked in water, and placed them over his heart, so that he should not expire quickly. His daughter exclaimed, "Father, that I should see you in this state!" He replied, "If it were I alone being burnt it would have been a thing hard to bear; but now that I am burning together with a Scroll of the Torah, He who will have regard for the plight of the Torah will have regard for my plight." His disciples called out, "Rabbi, what do you see?" He answered them, "The parchments are being burnt, but the letters are soaring on high." "Open your mouth," said they, "so that the fire can enter [and you will one should injure himself." The Executioner then said to him, "Rabbi, if I raise the flame and take away the tufts of wool from over your heart, will you cause me to enter into the life to come?" "Yes," he replied. "Promise me," he urged. So he promised him. He thereupon raised the flame and removed the tufts of wool from his heart, and he died quickly. The Executioner then threw himself into the fire and a *bath-kol* exclaimed, "Rabbi Haninah ben Teradion and the Executioner have been assigned to the world to come!" When Rabbi heard this he wept and said, "One may acquire eternal life in a single hour, another after many years."

Beruriah, the wife of Rabbi Meir, was a daughter of Rabbi Hanina ben Teradion. Said she to her husband, "I am ashamed to have my sister placed in a brothel." So he took a bagful of *denarii* and set out. If, thought he, she has not been subjected to anything wrong, a miracle will happen, but if she has committed anything wrong, there will be no miracle. Disguised as a knight, he came to her and said, "Prepare yourself for me." She replied, "The manner of women is upon me." "I am prepared to wait," he said. "But," she said, "there are many, many prettier than I am." He said to himself, that proves that she has done nothing wrong; she probably says this to all comers. He then went to her guard and said, "Hand her over to me." He replied, "I am afraid of the government." "Take this bagful of *denars*," said he, "use half to bribe your associates, and keep the other half for yourself." "And what shall I do when these run out?" he asked. "Then," he replied, "say 'O God of Meir answer me.' and you will be saved." "But," said he, "who can assure me of this?" Meir replied, "You will see now." There were some dogs around who bit anyone who incited them. He took a stone and threw it at them, and when they were about to bite he exclaimed, "O God of Meir answer me!" and they let him alone. The warder then handed her over to him. Eventually the matter became known to the government, and the guard on being brought for judgment was taken up to the gallows, when he exclaimed, "O God of Meir answer me!" They took him down and asked him what that meant, and he told them the incident that had happened. Then they engraved Rabbi Meir's likeness on the gates of Rome and proclaimed that anyone seeing a person resembling it should bring him there. One day some Romans saw him and ran after him, so he ran away and entered a harlot's house . . . and they said were this Rabbi Meir he would not have acted thus, and they let him go. He then arose and ran away and came to Babylon. . . .

-AVODA ZARA 18B

- 9 -

There were once some highwaymen in the neighborhood of Rabbi Meir who caused him a great deal of trouble. Rabbi Meir accordingly prayed that they should die. His wife Beruriah said to him, "How can you pray thus? Rather pray for them that they should repent, and there will be no more wicked." He did pray for them and they repented.

-BERAKHOT 9B

- 10 -

It has been taught: His name was not Rabbi Meir but Rabbi Nehorai. Then why was he called Rabbi Meir? Because he enlightened the Sages in the *halakhah*. His name in fact was not even Nehorai but Nehemiah, or as others say, Rabbi Eleazar ben Arak. The why was he called Nehorai. Because he enlightened the Sages in the *halakhah*. Rabbi declared: "The only reason why I am keener than my colleagues is that I saw the back of Rabbi Meir [note: his seat in the academy was behind Rabbi Meir as he lectured], but had I had a front view of him, I would have been keener still."

-ERUBIN 13B

- 11 -

He [the Emperor] sent Nero against them. As he was coming, he shot an arrow towards the east, and it fell in Jerusalem. He then shot one towards the west, and it fell in Jerusalem. He shot towards all four points of the compass, and each time it fell in Jerusalem. He said to a certain boy, "Repeat to me the last verse of Scripture you have learnt." He said, "*I will wreak vengeance on Edom through my people Israel.*" [Ezek. 25:14] He said, "The Holy One Blessed be He, desires to lay waste His House and to lay the blame on me." So he ran away and became a proselyte, and Rabbi Meir was descended from him.

-GITTIN 56A

- 12 -

Rabbi Meir used to deliver discourses on Sabbath evenings. There was a woman there in the habit of listening to him. Once the discourse lasted a long time, and she waited until the exposition was concluded. She went home and found that the candle had gone out. Her husband asked her, "Where have you been?" She answered, "I was sitting listening to the voice of the preacher." Said he to her, "I swear we will not let you enter here until you go and spit in the face of the preacher." She stayed away one week, a second, a third. Said her neighbors to her, "Are you still angry one with the other? Let us come with you to the discourse." As soon as Rabbi Meir saw them, he saw by means of the Holy Spirit what had happened, and said, "Is there a woman among you clever at whispering a charm over an eye?" The woman's neighbors said to her, "If you go and spit in his eye you will release your husband from his vow." When she sat down before him she became afraid of him, and said to him, "Rabbi, I am not expert at whispering an invocation over an eye." Said he to her, "For all that, spit in my face seven times, and I will be cured." She did so, and he said to her, "Go tell your husband, 'You told me to do it once, and I spat seven times.' " Said his disciples to him, "Should people thus abuse the Torah? Could you not have told one of us to whisper an invocation for you?" Said he to them, "Is it not good enough for Rabbi Meir to be like unto his Creator? For has not Rabbi Ishmael taught: Great is peace, since even of God's Ineffable Name, written though it be in sanctity, The Holy One blessed be He has said, 'Let it be blotted out in water for the purpose of making peace between husband and wife!' "

-MIDRASH LEVITICUS RABBAH, 9:9

- 13 -

Rabbi Meir used to say: From what source can we deduce that even an idolater who studies the Torah is equal to a High Priest? From the following verse—*You shall keep my laws and my rules, by the pursuit of which man shall live* [Lev. 18:5]—It does not say "If a Priest, Levite or Israelite do, he shall live by them," but, *man*. From this you may deduce that even a heathen who studies Torah is equal to a High Priest!

-AVODAH ZARAH 3A

- *14* -

Rabbi Samuel bar Nahmani said: I was seated on my Grandfather's shoulder going up from my town to Kfar hana via Bet She'an, and I heard Rabbi Simeon ben Eliezer say in Rabbi Meir's name, "And behold it was very good [should be read as] behold death is good."

SUPPLEMENT: CHAPTER EIGHT

Rabbinic Texts: Elisha ben Abuya

- 1 -

Aher mutilated the shoots. Of him Scripture says, *Don't let your mouth bring you into disfavor, and don't plead before the messenger that was in error* [Eccles. 5:5]. What does it refer to?—He saw that permission was granted to Metatron to sit and write down the merits of Israel. Said he: It is taught as a tradition that on high there is no sitting and no emulation and no back and no weariness. Perhaps—God forbid—there are two divinities. Thereupon they led Metatron forth, and punished him with sixty fiery lashes, saying to him, "Why did you not rise before him when you saw him?" Permission was then given to him to strike out the merits of Aher. A *Bath Kol* went forth and said, *Turn back, O rebellious children* [Jer. 3:2]—except Aher.

[Thereupon] he said: Since I have been driven forth from the world to come, let me go out and enjoy this world. So Aher went out into evil courses. He found a harlot and demanded her. She said to him, "Are you not Elisha ben Abuya?" But when he tore a radish out of its bed on the Sabbath and gave it to her, she said, "It is another [*Aher*]."

After his apostasy, Aher asked Rabbi Meir a question, saying to him, "What is the meaning of the verse, *The one no less than the other was God's doing* [Eccl. 7:14]?" He replied, "It means that everything that God created, he created also its counterpart. He created mountains, and created hills; he created seas and created rivers." Said Aher to him, "Rabbi Akiba, your Master, did not explain it thus, but as follows: He created righteous, and created wicked; He created the Garden of Eden and He created Gehinnom. Everyone has two portions, one in the Garden of Eden, and one in Gehinnom. The righteous man, being meritorious, takes his own portions and his fellow's portion in the Garden of Eden. The wicked man, being guilty, takes his own portion and his fellow's portion in Gehinnom." Rabbi Mahersheya said, "What is the Biblical proof for this? In the case of the righteous, it is written, *They shall have a double share in their land* [Isa. 61:7]. In the case of the wicked it is written, *And shatter them with double destruction* [Jer. 17:18]."

After his apostasy, Aher asked Rabbi Meir, "What is the meaning of the verse, *Gold or glass cannot match its value, nor vessels of fine gold be exchanged for it* [Job 28:17]?" He answered, "These are the words of the Torah, which are hard to acquire like vessels of fine gold, but are easily destroyed like vessels of glass." Said Aher to him, "Rabbi Akiba, your Master, did not explain it thus, but as follows: Just as vessels of gold and vessels of glass, though they be broken, have a remedy, even so a scholar, though he has sinned, has a remedy." Thereupon Rabbi Meir said to him, "Then you repent also!" He replied, "I have already heard from behind the Veil, *Turn back, rebellious children* [Jer. 3:14]—except Aher!"

-HAGIGAH 15A

- *2* -

Our Rabbis taught: Once Aher was riding on a horse on the Sabbath, and Rabbi Meir was walking behind him to learn Torah at his mouth. Said Aher to him, "Meir, turn back, for I have already, by the paces of my horse, measured a distance that exceeds the Sabbath limit." He replied, "You too turn back!" Aher answered, "Have I not already told you that I have already heard from behind the Veil, *Turn back, rebellious children*—except Aher." Rabbi Meir prevailed upon him and took him to a schoolhouse.

Aher said to a child, "Recite your verse for me." The child answered, *There is no safety, said the Lord, for the wicked* [Isa. 48:22]. He then took him to another schoolhouse. Aher said to a child, "Recite your verse for me." He answered, *Though you wash with natron and use much lye, your guilt is ingrained before me* [Jer. 2:22]. He took him to yet another schoolhouse, and Aher said to a child, "Recite your verse for me." He answered, *And you who are doomed to ruin, what do you accomplish by wearing crimson, by decking yourself in jewels of gold, by enlarging your eye with mascara? You beautify yourself in vain.* [Jer. 4:30] He took him to yet another schoolhouse until he took him to thirteen schools. All of them quoted in a similar vein. When he said to the last one, "Recite your verse for me," he answered, *"And to the wicked, God said, 'Who are you to recite My laws?'"* [Ps. 50:16] That child was a stutterer, so it sounded as though he answered "But to Elisha God said. ." [note: *lareshaim*. i.e. "to the wicked" came out as *l'Elisha*, i.e. "To Elisha] Some say that Aher had a knife with him, and he cut him up and sent him to the thirteen schools. But others say that he said, "Had I a knife in my hand I would have cut him up!"

-IBID. 15B

- *3* -

When Aher died, they said: Let him not be judged, nor let him enter the world to come. Let him not be judged, because he is engaged in the study of the Torah; nor let him enter the world to come, because he sinned. Rabbi Meir said, "It were better that he should be judged and that he should enter the world to come. When I die, I shall cause smoke to rise from his grave." [i.e. as a sign that he has been forgiven]. When Rabbi Meir died, smoke rose up from Aher's grave. . . .

-IBID.

- 4 -

Aher's daughter once came before Rabbi and said to him, "O Master, support me." He asked her, "Whose daughter are you?" She replied, "I am Aher's daughter." Said he, "Are there any of his children left in the world? Is it not written in Scripture, *He has no seed or breed among his people, no survivor where he once lived!*" [Job 18:19] She answered, "Remember his Torah and not his deeds." Immediately a fire came down and enveloped Rabbi's bench. Thereupon Rabbi wept, "If it be so on account of those who dishonor her [i.e. the Torah], how much more so on account of those who honor her!"

-IBID.

- 5 -

But how did Rabbi Meir learn Torah at the mouth of Aher? Behold Rabbi ben Bar Hana said that Rabbi Johanan said, "What is the meaning of the verse, *For the lip of a priest guard knowledge, and men seek rulings from his mouth; for he is a messenger of the Lord of Hosts?*" [Mal. 2:7] This means that if the teacher is like an angel of the Lord of Hosts, they should seek the Torah at his mouth, but if not, they should not seek the Torah at his mouth! Resh Lakish answered, "Rabbi Meir found a verse and expounded it as follows, *Incline your ear and listen to the words of the sages; pay attention to my wisdom.* It does not say 'to their wisdom', but 'to my wisdom.' " Rabbi Haninah said, "He deduced it from here, *Take heed, lass, and note, incline your ear; forget your people and your father's house* [Ps. 45:11]" These verses contradict one another! There is no contradiction: in the one case Scripture refers to an adult, in the other to a child. When Rabbi Dimi came to Babylon he said, "In the West [i.e. Land of Israel] they say: Rabbi Meir ate the date and threw the kernel away."

Raba expounded, "What is the meaning of the verse, *I went down to the nut grove to see the budding of the vale?* [Song of Songs 6:11]

Why are scholars likened to the nut? To tell you that just as in the case of the nut, though it be spoiled with mud and filth, yet its contents are not rejected, so in the case of a scholar, although he may have sinned, his Torah is not rejected."

-IBID.

- 6 -

But what of Aher? Greek song did not cease from his mouth. It is told of Aher that when he used to rise to go from the school-house, many heretical books used to fall from his lap . . .

-IBID.

- 7 -

Rabbah ben Shila once met Elijah. He said to him, "What is the Holy One, blessed be He, doing?" He answered, "He utters traditions in the name of all the Rabbis, but in the name of Rabbi Meir he does not utter." Rabbah asked, "Why?" "Because he learns traditions at the mouth of Aher," [was Elijah's reply] Said Rabbah to him, "But why? Rabbi Meir found a pomegranate; he ate the fruit within it and threw away the peel!" Elijah answered, "Now He says, Meir My son says 'When a man suffers, to what expression does the *Shekhinah* give utterance?—My head is heavy, my arm is heavy!' If the Holy one, blessed be He, is thus grieved over the blood of the wicked, how much more so over the blood of the righteous that is shed."

-IBID.

- 8 -

Rabbi Jacob said: There is not a single precept in the Torah whose reward is stated at its side which is not dependent on the resurrection of the dead. Thus, in connection with honoring parents it is written, *That you may fare well in the land that the Lord your God is assigning you* [Deut. 5:16]. In reference to the dismissal from the nest it is written, *In order that you may fare well and have a long life.* [Deut. 22:7] Now, if one's father said to him, "Climb this tree and bring me young birds," and he climbs the tree, dismisses the mother bird [note: as the Torah commands] and takes the young, and then falls from the tree and is killed—where is this man's happiness, and where is his prolonging of days? But *in order that you may fare well* means on the day that is wholly good, and *have a long life,* [means] on the day that is wholly long. [i.e. the world to come]

Yet perhaps there was no such happening? Rabbi Jacob saw an actual occurrence. . . . Rabbi Joseph said: "Had Aher interpreted this verse as *Rabbi Jacob, his daughter's son,* he would not have sinned. Now what happened with Aher? Some say he saw something of this nature. [i.e. someone being killed while performing a commandment from the Torah] Others say he saw the tongue of Huzpith the *Meturgeman* [one of the greatest homilists of his time] dragged along by a swine. He exclaimed, "The mouth that uttered pearls licks the dirt!" Thereupon he went forth and sinned.

-KIDDUSHIN 39B

- 9 -

Shortly thereafter Elisha fell ill. They came to Meir and told him, "Your teacher is dying." So he went to visit him, and said, "Will you not repent your heresy" "Will such repentance be accepted in heaven?" asked Elisha. "Certainly," replied Meir, "even at the last moment repentance is accepted." Thereupon Elisha began to weep, and weeping, he died.

-J. HAGIGAH II:1*

Glossary

Aboth d'Rabbi Nathan: abbr. ADRN: A homiletical exposition of the Mishnah, *Pirkei Aboth* [Ethics of the Fathers]. Found in the Minor Tractates of the Talmud in the Soncino Translation.

a fortiori: [cf. *kal vahomer* infra.] from a major premise.

Aher: Hebrew for "the other one." The name by which Elisha ben Abuyah was known after his apostasy.

aksaniah: inn, or place of lodging.

alef: first letter of the Hebrew alphabet.

Al Ghazali: Islamic philosopher [1058–1111], critic of Arab philosophers, such as Avicenna, who were influenced by Aristotle.

a minori: [cf. *kal vahomer* infra.] from a minor premise.

Ariadne's thread: Ariadne, daughter of Minos, helps Theseus escape from the Labyrinth, by giving him a thread that unwinds as he enters, and helps him escape.

Avodah Zarah: a tractate of the Babylonian Talmud that deals with idolatry and idolaters.

bat kol: [literally, "daughter of a voice," Hebrew] used in Talmud to mean a voice from heaven.

Baba Mezia: lit. "Middle Gate" A tractate of the Talmud dealing with problems of civil law.

Ben Sirah: author of Book of Wisdom [ca. 200 BCE] in Apocrypha. Also known as Ecclesiasticus.

Berakhah: [Hebrew] blessing.

Berakhot: a tractate of the Babylonian Talmud dealing with prayer.

beth: second letter of the Hebrew alphabet. Also means "house."

beth hamidrash: House of Study.

biryoni: rebel, outlaw; here referring to the Zealots in the War Party in the last days of the siege of Jerusalem. [70 CE]

Bnei Bathyra: Hebrew, Sons of Bathyra. Favored by Herod as heads of the Sanhedrin until Hillel unseated them.

daleth: fourth letter of the Hebrew alphabet; also means "door".

darash: Hebrew for search, interpret or explain.

darshan: exegete, homilist or preacher.

derasha: sermon, homily, or lecture.

deus absconsitus: Latin, hidden God or God who disappears.

denarii: denarius, a Roman coin.

ehad: Hebrew, one.

eisegesis: Greek, reading a meaning into the text.

Eighteen Benedictions: the core of Rabbinic prayer; also known as *amidah* [prayer said standing, or *shemoneh esrei* [the eighteen].

Erubin: lit. limits; a tractate of the Babylonian Talmud that deals with the limits on movement within a city on the Sabbath.

exegesis: Greek, deducing a meaning from the text.

Gehinnom: Hebrew, the Valley of Hinnom; in talmudic literature generally taken to refer to Hell.

Gemara: from the Aramaic root *g'mar*, to learn; the extension of the Mishnah through discussion of Sages that expands meaning of Mishnah and with it makes up the Talmud.

Genesis Rabbah: A midrash, i.e. homilies and text interpretations of the book of Genesis. A part of *Midrash Rabbah*.

Gimel: third letter of the Hebrew alphabet.

Ha'azinu: Hebrew, hearken or listen; the first word of the poem/sermon of Moses in Deuteronomy 32.

Hagigah: Hebrew, celebration; a tractate of the Babylonian Talmud which deals with pilgrimages to Jerusalem and festival offerings.

halakhah: Hebrew, the way or path; as technical term refers to deductions of law from Scripture, or consensus agreements by the Sages.

halizah: Hebrew, the technical term for the legal process whereby the closest kin of a childless widow avoids the necessity of complying with the Torah command. Cf. Ruth 4:1ff. See also: levirate.

hallel: Hebrew, praise; technical term for structured prayer of thanksgiving, composed of selected Psalms, and read in the synagogue service during the three Pilgrim Festivals, Passover, Shavuot and Sukkot.

Hanukah: Festival of Lights which occurs in December and celebrates the victory for the freedom of religion and the establishing of the Second Jewish Commonwealth achieved by the Maccabees in the second pre-Christian century. Hanukah is a Hebrew word that means "dedication."

Hasmonean: the family name of Mattathias and his Maccabean descendants.

Hashmatat haShass: Hebrew, censored passages of the Talmud. A collection, principally about Jesus and early Christians, removed from the Talmud by Christian censors, and later by Jewish self-censorship.

Hume: David Hume, a British skeptical philosopher of the late eighteenth century, who cast doubt of the theory of causation.

huppah: Hebrew, canopy; technical term for canopy used in Jewish weddings.

intercallation: the process of determining the extra month in the Jewish lunar calendar to balance out the differences between the lunar year of 355 days and the solar year of 365 days. This is done every third year.

kareth: Hebrew, death penalty.

ketubah: Hebrew, marriage contract.

ketubim: Hebrew, Writings. The third part of the Old Testament as arranged by Rabbinic Judaism. Contains the books: Psalms, Proverbs, Job, Song of Songs, Ruth, Lamentations, Ecclesiastes, Esther, Daniel, Ezra, Nehemiah and I & II Chronicles.

Ketubot: A tractate of the Talmud dealing with marriage contracts.

Kislev: The third month of the Jewish religious year, during which Hanukah occurs.

levirate: Refers to the law in the Torah that requires the closest male kin to marry the childless widow to provide posterity in the tribe, as described in Genesis 38 and Ruth 4. Cf. *halizah*.

Leviticus Rabbah: The midrash to the book of Leviticus.

lulav: Palm branch, with myrtle and willow attached, used during the Festival of Sukkot, together with the citron [etrog].

ma'aseh merkava: Hebrew, account of the Chariot. A technical term for early Jewish mystical studies.

Maccabees: Leaders of revolt against the Syrian-Greek rulers of Palestine in the first and second century BCE. The Maccabees eventually achieved independence. From 140 BCE to 40 BCE they ruled as kings. The term Maccabee is a Hebrew acronym: *Mi Kamokha Baelim YHWH* [Who is like you among the Mighty, O Lord!].

mallows: salted fish, e.g. herring, food for the poor. Hebrew: *maluhim*.

mamzer: Hebrew, bastard.

Meir: Hebrew, he who shed light.

meforash: Hebrew, explained, interpreted.

Messiah: Hebrew, annointed one. *Mashiah*.

metuentes: Latin, God fearers. Hebrew, *yi'ei Adonay*. Refers to gentiles in the Roman Empire who worshiped one God and observed the Sabbath but did not convert to Judaism.

meturgeman: Aramaic, interpreter, translator. Technical term for person who interpreted the Torah text from the Hebrew into Aramaic, the language of the people in Babylonia. This term also refers to the aide of the Sage who repeated aloud to the large group what the Sage spoke silently.

midrash: Hebrew, process of interpretation. Used as technical term to describe books containing homiletical interpretation of the Torah.

Midrash Rabbah: A collection of homilies and text interpretations of the Pentateuch and the books of Song of Songs, Ruth, Lamentations, and Esther.

min, minim [pl]: Hebrew, sect or sectarian. Used in the Talmud to describe either heretical sects within Judaism, or gnostics. This term is frequently used to describe early Christians.

minuth: Hebrew, heresy.

nasi: Hebrew, chief, leader. Technical term used to describe the head of the sanhedrin, or the head of the academy. The highest religious authority from the first century onward.

nazirite: in Biblical times, one who promised to abstain from wine, and from cutting one's hair, and devoting oneself to the service of God, e.g. Samuel or Samson. Cf. Numbers 6. Hebrew: *nazir*

nehorai: Aramaic, he who sheds light, or the enlightened one.

Nissan: The seventh month of the Jewish religious year, the first month of spring, during which time the Passover occurs.

oker harim: Hebrew, uprooter of mountains.

palanquin: a litter, in which a member of the nobility is carried by servants.

parasang: a Persian measurement of distance, equivalent to four miles.

Pentateuch: Greek, The Five, i.e. The Five Books of Moses. Translation from the Hebrew, *humash*.

Pesahim: Tractate of the Talmud dealing with the laws and customs of Passover.

Pharisee: From the Hebrew, *parush* meaning separated. The group within Judaism, that developed the idea of the Oral Law having equal authority with the Written Law, who became the shapers of Rabbinic Judaism. They translated prophetic ideals through legislation for everyday life. Their distinctive beliefs included: immortality of the soul, existence of angels, divine providence, freedom of will, and resurrection of the dead at the time of the coming of the messiah.

Phylacteries: Hebrew, *tefillin,* worn in daily morning worship, based on Exodus 13:1, 11; Deuteronomy 6:4–9; 11:13–21. These passages are written on parchment, placed in leather cases, with thongs, and worn on left arm and forehead.

Pirkei Avot: Hebrew for "Ethics of the Fathers," a short collection of aphorisms of Sages, and tracing the handing on of the tradition of authority from Moses at Sinai down through the generation of the Sages. A tractate of the Mishnah.

punic: adjective, pertaining to Phoenicians. The Wars of the Romans against the Carthaginians in the second century BCE were known as the Punic Wars.

Rashi: acronym for Rabbi Solomon ben Isaac, eleventh century commentator of the Bible and talmud. Rashi lived in Troyes, France.

reshit: Hebrew, first or beginning.

Sadducees: Sect of Temple priests and sympathizers; stressed Written Torah and the right of the priests to interpret it against the claims of the Pharisees for the equal validity of the Oral Law. They rejected belief in resurrection of the dead, immortality of the soul, angels and divine providence.

Sanhedrin: a term of Greek origin applied to the Supreme Court consisting of seventy-one Sages. The final arbiter of legal decisions stemming from Written and Oral Torah. Also the name of a Tractate of the Talmud that deals with the structure of the courts and the duties of judges.

Seder: Hebrew, order. Term applied to Passover eve meal when the story of the Exodus was recounted in a special order fixed in the Haggadah, the liturgical book for the Passover Seder arranged by the Sages.

Sextus Empiricus: codifier of Greek empiricism, who lived in the last half of the second century and the first quarter of the third century CE.

Shabbat: Hebrew, Sabbath.

Shema: Hebrew, listen, hear. Used to refer to the watchword of the Jewish faith: "Hear, O Israel, the Lord our God, the Lord is one."

Sifrei: Aramaic, the books. An early Midrash, halakhic commentary to the Books of Numbers and Deuteronomy, dating from the second century CE.

Sons of Bathyra: cf. B'nai Bathyra supra.

Sukkah: The booth in which the Jewish people were commanded to dwell during the week of Tabernacles.

Sukkot: The Festival of Tabernacles or Booths.

takanot: Hebrew for changes, or reforms; a technical term for changes in laws or customs decreed by Sages.

tallit: Hebrew, prayer shawl with ritual fringes.

tamid: Hebrew, technical term for daily sacrifice in the Temple.

tefillin: Hebrew for phylacteries. Cf. supra.

teku: Aramaic, acronym of phrase *tishbi yitaretz kushiot va-abayot,* i.e. The Tishbite [Elijah] will solve all unsolved problems in the future.

tosefta: Aramaic, supplement; additions to the Mishnah that appeared as supplements at the time of the appearance of the Mishnah.

tropaik: Greek, tropaixos; the value is half a denar. In Latin it was known as Victoriatus or Quinarius.

zugot: Hebrew, pairs.

zuz: Hebrew, a silver coin, equals one fourth of a shekel, or one denar.

Index

Gabriel, 37, 65, 136
Galilee, 93, 122, 166
Gamaliel, 42, 61, 127, 142, 155, 159, 174, 175, 179
Garden of Eden, 83, 113, 198
Gehinnom, 113, 198
Gemara, 58, 149, 185
Genesis, 91, 102, 122, 124, 148
Genesis Rabbah, 12, 33, 78, 135, 170, 191
Gittin, 64, 68, 155, 195
golden calf, 13
Gomorrah, 11
Gophna, 156
Gospels, 3, 8, 73
Graduate Theological Union, v
Greek(s), 7, 18, 24, 37, 40, 43, 94, 98, 194, 133, 158, 202
guerrillas, 16

Hadrian, 56, 93, 101, 106, 169, 171, 172
Hagigah, 13, 81, 83, 103, 111–114, 117, 159, 172, 181, 199, 203
halakhah, 8, 10, 45, 47, 52, 58, 74, 82, 88, 91, 101, 106, 149, 164, 165, 179, 186, 194
halizah, 186
Hamleta, 51
Haninah ben Abba, 183
Haninah ben Dosa, 158
Haninah ben Teradion, 105, 106, 192, 193, 201
Hannah, 88
Hanukkah, 37, 38, 133
Hanuth, 158
Harran, 117
Hashmatat Hashass, 80
Hasidim, 77
Hasmonean, 37, 38, 133
Hebrew, 122, 123
Herod, 30
Hezekiah, 100
High Priest, 30, 31, 36, 37, 79, 103, 104, 133, 139, 146, 160, 164, 196
Hillel, 3, 40, 41, 42, 44–57, 68–70, 73, 74, 83, 85, 87–90, 100, 104, 115, 133, 137, 141–149, 190
Historiae, 64
Hiyya bar Abba, 33, 127, 183, 186
Holy of Holies, 30, 64, 65, 155, 186
Homer, 25

Honi the Circle-Maker, 138
Horayot, 26
Hosea, 151
Hullin, 110
Hume, 54
Huna, 83, 126, 182, 191
Huzpith the Meturgeman (Interpreter), 110, 127, 203
Hyrcanus, 74, 75, 161, 162

Ibn Ezra, 118
Idumean, 30
India, 24
Institut fuer Juedisch-Christliche Forschung, 1
Instant Messianism. *See* Short Range Messianism
Isaac, 82, 100, 108, 190
Isaac ben Abdimi, 142, 181
Isaiah, 13, 101, 119, 154, 155, 174, 198, 200
Ishmael, 101, 155, 191
Islam, 16, 49, 67
Israel, Israeli, 8, 104, 105, 111, 114, 123, 136, 137, 139, 144, 145, 151, 171, 175, 182, 198, 201

Jacob, 82, 95, 100, 108, 190
Jacob of Kfar Sekania, 79, 164
Jacob, Rabbi, 110, 203
Jannai. *See* Alexander Jammai
Jeremiah, 11, 19, 20, 21, 29, 47, 56, 66, 67, 85, 108, 119, 120, 122, 154
Jeremiah, Rabbi, 34, 73, 135, 165, 172, 174, 198, 200
Jeroboam II, 21
Jerusalem, 3, 17, 20, 30, 55, 60–66, 69, 70, 73, 77, 88, 92, 104, 105, 107, 108, 111, 123, 128, 134, 137, 152–157, 161, 180, 195
Jerusalem Talmud, 83, 97, 101, 112, 127
Jesus, 14, 15, 42, 78–80, 134, 164
Jews, Jewish, 55, 61, 62, 79, 82, 84, 88, 92–95, 97–100, 103, 107, 108, 111, 116, 117, 119, 123
Jewish Christians, 61
Jezebel, 28
Joab, 123
Job, 59, 107, 149, 176, 178, 201
Johanan, 33

A000015121349